THE ENEMIES BEHIND THE SCENE - V

BREAKING UNKNOWN CURSES

With Over 300 Uncommon Prayers That

Daramola Joel Odunayo

Copyright © J.O. Daramola

Tel: 08033275896, 07028206482

ISBN: 9798368209029

Published by

CHRIST THE REDEEMER'S MINISTRIES

1-9, Redemption Way, P.M.B. 1088, Ebute Metta, Lagos, Nigeria.

Unless otherwise stated, all scriptural quotation are from the Authorized King James Version of the Holy Bible.

Printed in Nigeria by: **CRM PRESS**

KM 46 Lagos-Ibadan Expressway, CRM Shopping Complex, Back of Old Auditorium, Redemption Camp,

Tel: 08077833792, 08069452037

E-mail: crmpress@yahoo.com

TABLE OF CONTENT

DEDICATION

This book is dedicated to our Lord Jesus Christ; my Saviour and the Holy Spirit, my senior partner in life and ministry and my heavenly Father, the Almighty God (YAHWEH) and to my biological father, Late Pa Solomon Kolawole Daramola, also to everyone that attends 'Power Service' our weekly breakthrough and deliverance service in various locations.

ACKNOWLEDGMENT

I've been blessed and surrounded by committed people over the years and they remain faithful supporting this vision. Thank you very much to you all.

To all who laboured to bring this book to fruition, thank you.

Much thanks to my wonderful wife, Pastor (Mrs.) C.O. Daramola and my daughter, Esther Daramola for careful transcription, and proofreading of the manuscript, laying the groundwork for this book. Bro Sunday Aremu, thank you, again for proofreading, editing and graphic illustrations of the messages so to make it easily readable.

Much thanks to Pastor Aremu Adegoke for his careful and patient final works to make this book available to the readers.

God bless you all. Your help brought this to publication. Thank you very much.

INTRODUCTION

Curses are mentioned over 200 times in the Scriptures. God Himself was the first to pronounce curses on the earth, on Eve's fertility and upon the serpent. Curses are not just a primitive superstition, they are spiritual pronouncements recorded in the Scriptures that profoundly affect the very structure of reality in some way.

A curse could be explained to be a set of words issued for destructive purposes.

an evil statement said or invoked upon someone as a result of sin or one evil act that is done.

an invocation of harm or injury to come upon one; it could be direct or indirect. The direct one is a curse that someone receives on himself, while the indirect is the one that is inherited by birth, marriage, location, or association of any kind.

a commission given to Satan to limit the life of a person an invisible spiritual barrier.

Curse has many names - spell, sanctions or curses. The father of Reuben placed a sanction upon him; Goliath cursed David (1 SAMUEL

17:43); Haman placed a spell upon Mordecai (Esther 3:7).

A curse is a set of words issued for destructive purposes.

A curse is an evil statement said or invoked upon someone as a result of sin or one evil act that is being done.

Curse is an invocation of harm or injury to come upon one; a curse could be direct or indirect. The direct one is a curse that someone receives on himself while the indirect one is the one that one inherits, marries into or enters by moving into a cursed environment or office etc.

A curse is a commission given to Satan to limit the life of a person.

The enemy may decide to take 20 years out of the life of a person by issuing a curse.

A curse is a direct opposite of blessing

A weapons of darkness. Isaiah 54:17.

An evil utterance or pronouncement.

An invisible spiritual barrier.

An invisible hand directing the affairs of a person's life.

Labouring under a closed heaven.

They invisible ropes binding a person's destiny.

Supervised by strongmen and demons.

An instrument of limitation.

A curse is a force of retardation. So, (if you dream of your primary school days , secondary school days or that somebody converted you to a housemaid or houseboy or slave, then you need to break the curse of retardation).

Some have authority over your situation; unfortunately they use it wrongly. Do you know that it is you and God that have the final say over your matter? Remember, 1Chr. 4:9-10 is about Jabez life. When her mother misused her authority and he reversed it. Again, in 1 Sam. 4:17-21, Ichabod did nothing about his own situation.

What then is a curse?

A curse is:

A weapons of darkness. Isaiah 54:17.
An evil utterance or pronouncement.
An invisible spiritual barrier.

The opposite of a blessing.

An invisible hand directing the affairs of a person's life.

Laboring under a closed heaven.

They invisible ropes binding a person's destiny.

Supervised by strongmen and demons.

An instrument of limitation.

labouring under a closed heaven.

Curses and creation

The world was created by the word of God and is held together by the power of His word (Genesis 1; Hebrews 1:1-3; Colossians 1:17-20). Thus, God's words can change creation. Jesus cursed a fig tree, representing barren Israel, to shrivel up. Blessings and curses are, first of all, God's words that operate at this fundamental level of creation and "tilt the playing field" of life one way or another.

Secondly, curses and blessings can be from evil spirits or flow from the human spirit. Goliath's curses against David were "by his gods" (1 Samuel 17:43) and were ineffective. The David-and-Goliath encounter was a power encounter of one spiritual system against the other and both contenders came in the name of their respective deities.

Shamans and magicians, such as Balaam were hired to curse people in Old Testament times and still do this today. Though curses from evil sources are much less powerful than curses from

God, they were still feared and were able to do much damage. There are 22 references exhorting believers not to curse others. Curses are finally ended in the new creation (Rev 22:3).

CHAPTER ONE: THE ORIGIN OF BLESSINGS AND CURSES

The origin of blessings and curses is found in the Book of Genesis. The first blessing was upon the living creatures which were told to "be fruitful and multiply" (Genesis 1:22). When God made mankind, He also blessed them saying, "be fruitful and multiply, replenish the earth, subdue it" and added a fifth blessing, "have dominion over..." (Genesis 1:28). These five basic blessings formed the basis of all future blessings, such as the Abrahamic blessings, and their reversal formed the basis of all future curses, such as those in Genesis 3.

Fruitfulness is the ability to joyfully express your inner nature and feel that which you are doing is truly creative, worthwhile and significant. Its opposite is a pain in creation, especially barrenness.

Multiplication is exponential increase - increasing as in 2, 4, 8, 16, 32, 64, 128 not additively as in 2 , 4, 6, 8, 10. Multiplication is a huge increase in productivity for a small increase in effort. Its opposite is frustration and futility; putting in a huge effort for little or no reward.

Replenishing the earth calls for the human race to spread ass they multiply. That is, they are not to keep themselves at a spot since the world God created for them is theirs, big, vast and adventurous.

Subduing the earth, this part of the blessing gives man the ability to control what is in the earth, tame what is tameable, and it accounts for the possible inventions that the human race has come up with so far.

Authority to rule over means, dignity, headship, authority; the ability to be ascendant; to be the head, not the tail. Its opposite is being humbled, to eat the dirt, to be crushed and humiliated, to be unable to rise.

In Genesis 3, we see the first curses in operation. The woman was made unfruitful, the man was made to work in futility and the serpent was told to eat the dirt. The three things that make life good were reversed. Life became unbearable. Thus, when we are cursed, we find life very difficult indeed. No matter how hard we try to rise, we never quite make it. Times and times again, we get to the brink of success, only to have it snatched away.

Curses can affect health, particularly reproductive health. They can affect earning power and they can affect our ability to have authority and command over our lives and people who are cursed may have to endure a life long humiliation.

And the men of the city said unto Elisha, Behold, I pray thee, the situation of this city is pleasant, as my lord seeth: but the water is naught, and the ground barren.

And he said, Bring me a new cruse, and put salt therein. And they brought it to him.

And he went forth unto the spring of the waters, and cast the salt in there, and said, Thus saith the LORD, I have healed these waters; there shall not be from thence any more death or barren land. So the waters were healed unto this day, according to the saying of Elisha which he spake.

(II Kings 2:19-22)

As the bird by wandering, as the swallow by flying, so the curse causeless shall not come. (Proverbs 26:2).

And if a soul sin, and commit any of these things which are forbidden to be done by the commandments of the Lord; though he wist it not, yet is he guilty, and shall bear his iniquity. (Lev. 5:17)

Hear, O earth: behold, I will bring evil upon this people, even the fruit of their thoughts, because they have not hearkened unto my words, nor to my law, but rejected it. (Jer. 6:19)

Curses can be issued against a person, place, or thing. Many individuals are labouring under curses. Anything can be cursed including names, individuals, families, cities, nations, and even continents.

Curses mostly target three major areas.

These are the head, which represents your destiny;

The hands which represent your handiwork; and

The legs represent your establishment.

SOURCES OF CURSES

Curses originate from various sources. The three major sources are:

Curses from God: An example is the one that God put of Cain for killing his brother Abel. Genesis 3:14.

Curses from Satan: These are curses that originate from satan and his agents such as idol, witchcraft, familiar spirit, and marine powers. (Evil spirits that is provokes)

Curses from man: A good example is the one that Jacob put on his son Reuben for sleeping with his wife. Genesis 49:3-4. Another is the curse that David put on Joab for killing Abner. 2 Samuel 3:29. Self (unknowns) include our conduct (Violation of Covenant, idolatry, participation in the occult)

Most curses fight as a result of broken covenants between people. If the terms of the agreement are not kept then sanctions kick in. These sanctions often manifest as curses. The Bible clearly teaches that there is always a reason why curses kick into place. Proverbs 26:2. There are spirits and demons attached to curses to enforce them.

The destiny of man is a progressive destiny, however certain forces arises to hinder the flow of progress in life. One of these forces is the unknown curse this type of curse limits their victims.

The following could be a curse. Note that I did not say that it is a curse, but 'could be'. This is because some situations may not necessarily be a curse.

It could be a curse when all your efforts and total inputs yield no result.

When you are going through mysterious experiences

When you notice that you are always moving backward, instead of forward

When you are experiencing persistent failure in everything you put your hands upon

When men and women who are supposed to be winners are woeful failures

When you are governed and controlled by the powers that are contrary to your own will

When inexplicable hatred comes up between a husband and his wife

When a brilliant person suddenly becomes dull

When a child that was previously gentle and obedient suddenly becomes stubborn and violent

When a rich person suddenly becomes poor

When uncontrollable temper suddenly surfaces

When you often feel rejected, inferior, depressed, insecure, and confused and always fall into self-pity

When you have an unstable sexual appetite.

When you experience sicknesses that are associated with a dry or wet session

When your personal trials refuse to come to an end.

When you continue to battle with problems, periodically

When you are always fed by satanic agents in your dream

When the problems in your life begin to multiply

When you experience constant broken engagements and disappointments.

When you dream of communicating with a dead person.

When you have a lot of money, but no peace

When in your family some brothers threaten to kill one another.

When you run in circles because forces of retrogression have set in

When you do your best and nobody appreciates you

Perhaps you are like Peter who was fishing and catching nothing. You could be labouring under a curse.

Many people are suffering from bad diseases that doctors cannot understand.

In some families, every first daughter would have a child without a husband and some, none of the women settles down.

For some, the women feed their husbands; even if the man had a job before the marriage, he would lose it after.

Never take anything for granted because there are certain issues in life that are actually curses

These are the biblical generation or natural curses

THESE CAN BE GROUPED INTO:

There are different types of curses which are often determined by their source or origin. They include the following that are listed below:

Ancestral curses which come through the bloodline.

Generational curses. These go from one generation to another in a family. Examples are heart disease, blood disease, and insanity.

Personal curses which are self-imposed or inflicted curses. Examples are swearing to one's own hurt or stealing from others.

Tribal curses. These are curses originating from your tribe or your home town.

International curses. These are curses that cut across continents.

You can inherit a curse (11king 5:27; 11Samuel 3:28-29)

You can marry into a curse (Hosea 9:14)

Location curses can come via location (1king 16:34)

Opposition curses can come through opposition (Number 22:6)

A curse may be returned to you i. e. cursing somebody that has not offended you, yet is more powerful than you are. In essence, the person has the power to revoke the curse you placed on him
so that whatever curse placed upon him/her will surely come back to the one that placed the curse.

Doing God's work with deception can bring a curse upon you (Jer. 48:10).

Idolatry: Serving and worshiping false gods, occult involvement, special baths in the sea, etc. could place a person under a curse. A person whose ancestors were involved in these things also comes under the curse, even though he did not do so himself. Out of their activities, some forefathers put their descendants under a curse. Until anyone concerned releases himself from the curse and breaks it, he will not be free. Idolatry or involvement in occult practices puts one under automatic curses. There is no prayer that can help such a person, except he repents.

Curses could be Generational

Curses from Generation Sin: There are negative effects of generational sin. Eve's rebellion led to pain in childbirth. (Gen 3:16) Abraham lied, Jacob lied. (Gen 20:2, 27:7) Generational curses can affect a nation. (Is 24) Curses can affect increase "You sow a wind and reap a whirlwind. (Hosea 8:7) Children suffer from the sins of their fathers. (II Sam 12:1-19) Also see: Deut 5:9 23:2,3 38:45,46, 58,59; Num 14:18; Lev 26:40-42; Ex 25:3,4 34:67; Isaiah 65:6,7; Dan 9:16; Matt 2:7:25; John 9:1-2

 "Our fathers sinned, and are no more; it is we who have borne their iniquities." (Lamentations 5:7)

Generational curses can turn kings to slaves, can convert fertile land to desert, can convert goldmine to dunghill, can turn eagle to chick and hero and zero.

When Naaman came to Elisha, he instructed him to go and wash in the pool. This particular story is very important as it deals with generational issues. The reason why Elisha asked him to deep himself SEVEN times correlates to the fact that the disease had been in operation for seven generations. Each deep represents one generation and that was why he saw no effect until he got to the 7th deep. To ascertain these facts, when Gehazi misbehaved, Elisha's curse on him confirms the fact that this disease was a generational issue.

Don't choose to pass curses to your children, pass blessing to them. Some families have been cursed with poverty from generation to generation. If you are operating under a curse, nothing will work for you. You continue to move from one sickness to another.

In some families, financial failures, laziness, sudden death from stray bullets, horrible dreams, uncontrollable anger, having dangerous desires, worries, divorce, gambling and debt are the curses facing them.

The good thing is that Jesus died on the cross and when he said it is finished all those curses finished.

A CURSE ALWAYS HAS A CAUSE

The word "curse" means a malevolent appeal to a supernatural being for harm to come to somebody or something, or the harm that is thought to result from this or to appeal malevolently to a supernatural being for harm to come to somebody or something.

If a curse is working in our life, it will always have a cause. Proverbs 26:2 says

'Like a sparrow in its flitting and a swallow in its flying so a curse without a cause CANNOT alight.'

By reading Deuteronomy 28 and Leviticus 26, one can find many curses (and blessings) listed. It would do well for each one of us to examine which curses (and blessings) are applicable in our own lives.

Unfortunately, there are those who do not believe a Christian can be under a curse. All they need to do is read I Corinthians 11:27-31 where it says a believer who takes the Lord's Supper with unconfessed and unrepented sin in his life, can be weak, sick, and even die.

'Wherefore whosoever shall eat this bread, and drink this cup of the Lord, unworthily, shall be guilty of the body and blood of the Lord. But let a man examine himself, and so let him eat of that bread, and drink of that cup. For he that eateth and drinketh unworthily, eateth and drinketh damnation to himself, not discerning the Lord's body. For this cause many are weak and sickly among you, and many sleep (deceased/die). `

"My people are destroyed for lack of knowledge: because thou hast rejected knowledge." (Hosea 4:6)

There are many who mistakenly believe because these verses are found in the Old Testament, they are not relevant today. However, 2 Timothy 3:15-18 (as well as many other verses) dispels this lie. It says:

"All Scripture is inspired by God and profitable for teaching, for reproof, for correction, for training in righteousness; so that the man of God may be adequate, equipped for every good work."

Sadly, whether they choose to believe it or not, they do exist in a believer's life. Curses come about through iniquity and iniquity comes about from sin. In other words, when an individual transgresses God's law, then it creates an iniquity in him and that iniquity is, therefore, passed to his children. It causes a weakness or bent toward that certain behavior or you may continuously yield toward that temptation which is passed from generation to generation. That certain iniquity will continue to affect that particular bloodline until someone in the bloodline takes accountability for it, confesses it as sin and appropriates the blood of Jesus over it.

"Thou shalt not bow down thyself to them [idols], nor serve them: for I the LORD thy God am a jealous God, visiting the iniquity of the fathers upon the children unto the third and fourth generation of them that hate me."

(Exodus 20:5)

I Corinthians 3:9 says:

"For we are God's fellow workers; you are God's field, God's building."

Isaiah 5:7 says:

"The vineyard of the LORD of hosts is the house of Israel and the men of Judah His delightful plant."

And we are instructed in Hosea 10:12 to

"Sow with a view to righteousness, reap in accordance with kindness; break up your fallow ground, for it is time to seek the LORD until He comes to rain righteousness on you."

Curses and blessings are often like seeds planted in a garden. They may be evil or good. They are planted deep within the soil of your soul (your mind, will and emotions). Seeds planted can come from your childhood or from your fore-fathers, planted within you before you are born, either producing good or bad fruits.

Certainly each one of us can be sure there is a curse working in his or her life when we find ourselves being overcome, defeated, bitter, angry, hurt, fearful, terrorized, sick, mentally ill, addicted, depressed, confused, discouraged...etc., and in the midst of this attack, there appears to be no healing or permanent relief for our problem. If this be the case, we need to seek God for the unresolved hidden cause(s) of the curse. The cause may not only be our own sin, but also the generational iniquity of our fore-fathers. We must confess our own personal sin (what we are reaping) and that of our fore-fathers.

"We acknowledge, O LORD, our wickedness, and the iniquity of our fathers: for we have sinned against thee."

(Jeremiah 14:20)

Praise God that when the sin behind the curse is dealt with (confessed and cut at the root), victory as well as healing will come. I often tell others that this is one major reason why going to the world for help (to hang in there) does not remove the curse or the demon(s) behind the curse. It is likened to removing the spider web, but allowing the spider to remain! It simply puts a big temporary worldly band aide on a spiritual problem!

If a curse is working in your life, there is a cause. If you are not careful to observe all the words of this law which are written in this book, to fear this honoured and awesome name, the LORD your God, then the LORD will bring extraordinary plagues on you and your descendants, even severe and lasting plagues, and miserable and chronic sicknesses (Deut. 28:58-60) This scripture clearly indicates sicknesses stem from curses. Simply put, demons carry out the curses and holy angels carry out the blessings.

2 Timothy 3:12 says:

"Yea, and all that will live godly in Christ Jesus shall suffer persecution."

However, the Bible also promises that even in the midst of persecution, we can be victorious! Praise God! It does not matter, whatever happens to us, regardless of what we suffer or go through, all of it is for the purpose of conforming us into the image of Christ! We CAN have overcoming victory. We can turn the wrong responses and attitudes around and manifest the character and nature of Jesus.

"Who shall lay anything to the charge of God's elect? It is God that justifieth. Who is he that condemneth? It is Christ that died, yea rather, that is risen again, who is even at the right hand of God, who also maketh intercession for us. Who shall separate us from the love of Christ? Shall tribulation, or distress, or persecution, or famine, or nakedness, or peril, or sword? As it is written, for thy sake we are killed all the day long; we are accounted as sheep for the slaughter. Nay, in all these things we are more than conquerors through him that loved us. For I am persuaded, that neither death, nor life, nor angels, nor principalities, nor powers, nor things present, nor things to come, nor height, nor depth, nor any other creature, shall be able to separate us from the love of God, which is in Christ Jesus our Lord." (Romans 8:33-39)

The difference between a fiery dart from the enemy and a curse is this: If it is just a fiery dart, taking up the shield of faith (being in God's refuge through dying to the flesh) dispels the attack of the enemy and victory is won.

"For You (God) have been a defense for the helpless, A defense for the needy in his distress, A refuge from the storm, a shade from the heat; for the breath of the ruthless Is like a rain storm against a wall."

(Isaiah 25:4)

"They that trust in the LORD shall be as mount Zion, which cannot be removed, but abideth forever. As the mountains are round about Jerusalem, so the LORD is round about his people from henceforth even forever. For the rod (dart) of the wicked shall not rest (stay, remain, abide) upon the lot of the righteous; lest the righteous put forth their hands unto iniquity. Do good, O LORD, unto those that be good, and to them that are upright in their hearts. As for such as turn aside unto their crooked ways, the LORD shall lead them forth with the workers of iniquity: but peace shall be upon Israel (the Church)." (Psalm 125:1-5)

"Thou wilt keep him in perfect peace, whose mind is stayed on thee: because he trusteth in thee."

(Isaiah 26:3)

"And the rain descended, and the floods came, and the winds blew, and beat upon that house;

and it fell not: for it was founded upon a rock."
(Jesus minus our idol(s). (Matthew 7:25)

"When a man's ways please the Lord, it makes
even his enemies to be at peace with him."
(Proverbs 16:7)

"A rebellious man seeks only evil so a cruel
messenger will be sent against him." (Proverbs
17:11)

"He who dwells in the secret place of the Most
High God shall abide under the shadow and
protection of the Almighty... "

"Because we make the Lord our refuge, even the
Most High our habitation, no evil will befall us and
no plague will come neigh our dwelling." (Psalms
91:1,11)

"Where then does wisdom come from? And where
is the place of understanding? Thus it is hidden
from the eyes of all living and concealed from the
birds of the sky" [Satan and his demons]. (Job
28:20-21)

"But thou, O LORD, be merciful unto me, and
raise me up, that I may requite them. By this I
know that thou favourest me, because mine

enemy doth not triumph over me."   (Psalms 41:10-11)

"Arise, O' LORD, disappoint him, cast him down: deliver my soul from the wicked which is

THY SWORD."

(Psalm 17:13)

A good way to describe our dilemma could be likened to a house with windows wide open, giving entrance to the enemy. As each window is closed through repentance, the enemy's entry way is being closed off. No longer does he have a legal right, except in the areas where the windows are left open. The Lord does not show us all the open windows (hidden places) at once; only those He has appointed next on His sanctifying list.

God drives the enemy out little by little (window by window). He uses the problems in our lives, (if we are wise enough to ask Him) not only for the purpose of conforming us into His image, but also to reveal unresolved issues. As those issues crop up, He expects us to deal with them heads on. Remember, Jesus already won the victory for us at Calvary and paid the price for our sanctification; but in order for us to work it out, (totally by His grace) it takes a lifetime.

"Wherefore, my beloved, as ye have always obeyed, not as in my presence only, but now much more in my absence, work out your own salvation (deliverance from the molestation of the enemy) with fear and trembling."

(Philippians 2:12)

Exodus 23:27-30 confirms that sanctification is a process. It says:

"I will send my fear before thee, and will destroy all the people to whom thou shalt come, and I will make all thine enemies turn their backs unto thee. And I will send hornets before thee which shall drive out the Hivite, the Canaanite, and the Hittite, from before thee (enemies). I will not drive them out from before thee in one year; lest the land become desolate, and the beast of the field multiply against thee. By little and little I will drive them out from before thee, until thou be increased, and inherit the land."

Be encouraged! If you are not into wilful sin and things appear not be going as expected, be mindful that God is not mad at you. It simply means that there are issues that He wants you to see about yourself or from the generations before you. He loves you so much. It is necessary He cleans you up for your highest good and for His greatest glory! His eyes are too pure to look upon and tolerate our sin. Those whom the Lord loves he disciplines, and he scourges every son whom he receives (Hebrews 12:6)

SOURCES OF CURSES

Curses originate from various sources. The three major sources are:

Curses from God: An example is the one that God put of Cain for killing his brother Abel. Genesis 3:14.

Curses from Satan: These are curses that originate from satan and his agents such as idol, witchcraft, familiar spirit, and marine powers.

Curses from man: A good example is the one that Jacob put on his son Reuben for sleeping with his wife. Genesis 49:3-4. Another is the curse that David put on Joab for killing Abner. 2 Samuel 3:29.

Humans enemies or Self

God

Evil spirits that are provoked

Covenant that is violated

Human

Self

our conduct of idolatry or participation in the occult

HOW DO CURSES ENTER INTO A MAN'S LIFE?

Curses may come upon someone because of his/her own conduct or involvement in

idolatry, participation in the occult, prostitution, fornication, sexual immorality, adultery, theft, injustice, direct defiant disobedience to God in an important area, and involvement in secret societies with rituals and vows.

Curses may be aimed at you by others because of hatred, envy, greed, jealousy, use of magic, spiritual conflict and the desire for revenge.

In some cases, parents curse their children, particularly the first-born son, in order to attain power in a deal with Satan or his representatives.

This is said to occur in Masonic rituals.

THE MYSTERY AND EFFECTS OF CURSES

The ignorance of man about a curse does not disturb its work. It even makes it more dangerous, but if you know that there is a curse upon you, you can quickly pray and fast about it. However, can you pray for what you are not aware of? No man will be justified for being ignorant, for ignorance is not an excuse. Ignorance is an agent of death which can cut one's life short. The problem many people have today is lack of knowledge (Hosea 4: 6). They don't know what to do, how to do it, and when to do it; and as a result of this, they are living a stagnant life. 1 king 16:34, Joshua 6:26-, 2kimgs 2:19-22.

Curses, spells or sanctions are of the devil and are not in line with God's plans for you. It could be that somebody, either dead or living, is responsible for it. There are different kinds of curses, spells or sanctions - known curses or unknown curses; inherited curses or direct curses; location curses; move into or trade into (sex); association curse or hereditary (city, town and nation curse), but what I know is that the curses upon you can turn into blessings (Ps. 109:28).

Being cursed is a terrible thing in one's life i. e. if a curse or sanction is placed on a student, no matter how brilliant he/she may be, he/she will not pass examinations. Many houses are under curses and nobody is ever willing to rent them. Many single brothers and sisters are under spells and sanctions to the extent that nobody approaches them for a relationship. Many marriages are barren because it is under a spell or curse (Hosea 9:14).

A curse is a tragedy that moves from generation to generation; you have to understand that. This is why we have a lot of educated illiterate around. Their chains of degrees cannot help them. Education is not an ability to nullify curses or the ability to defeat the forces limiting your life.

A family weakness can move from generation to generation. In some families, it is the curse of premature death. God said to Eli that no man in his family would enter his grave with grey hair. There are families like that. There are some families where their members never rise above a particular level. In Joshua 9:23, we see the curse that was put upon a whole tribe. It says, "Now, therefore, ye are cursed, and there shall none of you be freed from being bondmen, and hewers of wood and drawers of water for the house of my God."

Therefore, a curse is a terrible thing. It has a backing force and what you can call an enforcing spirit.

Escape by physical relocation is not the answer, but spiritual relocation. Physical relocation does not stop a curse, except it is locational curse like the one in Mark 8:22-.

A family or community can be in a position where it never produces a great person. There are communities where you cannot find any educated man.

Curses are real and, in some cases, they are even lethal; Ezekiel talks of magic charms that hunted lives (Ezekiel 13:18-20). Curses are on the rise in the Western culture as people dabble more and more in the occult and in organizations where people take secret oaths that invoke curses. Emotionally, curses produce deep confusion and despair and an inability to think straight.

If your life is affected by sterility, barrenness, constant lack of success and failure to gain any sort of ascendancy, no matter how hard you try, then a curse may be in operation. If you think this may be the case, then do some research on your life and family history and take the matter before the Lord!

Delay in life - when every lady in a particular family finds it difficult to find a husband, or they are not able to stay with one man or their husbands or all the girls are prostitutes, or all the men have troublesome wives.

When somebody is experiencing mental or emotional breakdown, stubborn sicknesses, sickness without any medical diagnosis, regular child death, bearing illegitimate children

When you are experiencing financial problems all the time. Although he comes in contact with money, he is duped by robbers or invests in the wrong business, such a person is under a curse.

If you are experiencing activities without productivity; faithful but forgotten in the time of promotion

Being prone to accidents, accumulation of problems and history of suicide or sudden deaths are all signs of presence of curses.

Evil dreams; dealing with evil dreams is another way to trouble your trouble. Any dream that you keep having and is setting you back, you should deal with it. All the dreams of climbing and never getting to the top; dreams of running around and getting nowhere are a way of God trying to tell you that something wrong is going on. You need to wake up and start to fight.

Curses or spells cast on persons can lead to confusion, often involving a "floating" mental state; sometimes a loss of memory during which actions are performed and weakening the person's will, so they are easily seduced/manipulated etc.

Sickness beyond medical diagnosis - A cursed fellow often tormented with internal sickness like a sharp stabbing pain in the head or abdomen that is without medical explanation and which is emotionally distressing. Drug addiction may sometimes be associated with occult activity and casting of spells against people.

All round stagnancy. Nothing works in business, career, ministry, marriage and other areas.

Broken marriages and relationships.

Diseases and infirmities.

Mistakes and errors. Take wrong steps leading to unpardonable mistakes.

Wrong location: They ensure that you are at the wrong place and that you arrive at your place of blessing late so the blessing fly over your head.

Attracts hatred, rejection, and disappointment where there should be appointment.

Failure where there should be success: Especially failure at the edge of life changing breakthroughs.

Rising and falling: Get and lose syndrome. This makes it impossible to retain good things.

Demotion where there should be promotion.

Its Cripples a person's life: Amputates and diverts destinies.

Violent, tragic, or untimely death.

Profitless hard-work. This is because the person is laboring under a closed heaven.

SYMPTOMS OR SIGNS OF CURSE IN ONE'S LIFE?

Delayed in life, when every lady in a particular family finds it difficult to find a husband, or they are not able to stay with one man or their husbands or all the girls are prostitutes, or all the men are have troublesome wives

When somebody is experiencing mental or emotional breakdown, stubborn sicknesses, sickness without any medical diagnosis, regular child death, bearing illegitimate children

When you are experiencing financial problems all the time. Although he comes in contact with money, he is duped by robbers or invests in the wrong business, such a person is under a curse.

If you are experience activities without productivities, faithful but forgetting in the time of promotion

Being prone to accidents, accumulation of problems and history of suicide or sudden deaths are all signs of curses.

Evil dreams; Dealing with evil dreams is another way to trouble your trouble. Any dream that you keep having and is setting you back, you should deal with it. All the dreams of climbing and never getting to the top, all the dreams of running around and getting nowhere, is a way of God trying to tell you that something wrong is going on. You need to wake up and start to fight.

Curse or Spells cast on persons can leads confusion, often involve a "floating" mental state, sometimes a loss of memory during which actions are performed and a weakening of the person's will so they are easily seduced/manipulated etc.

Sickness beyond medical diagnosis; a curse fellow often torment with internal sickness like a sharp stabbing pain in the head or abdomen that is without medical explanation and which is emotionally distressing. Drug addiction may sometimes be associated with occult activity and casting of spells against people.

Example biblical examples:

In 1 King 16:34, a man woke up to help the city to build a wall that has collapsed for a long time. Suddenly he lost his sons, as a result of the unknown curse place on Jericho by Joshua many years before then Joshua 6:26 (2 Kings 2:19) thanks God for Elisha that nullified all the curses upon Jericho.

A man comes into a city for trade and because that city was under a curse (Matt. 11:21), He became blind. (Mark 8:22-26).

Generational curses can turn kings to slaves, can convert fertile land to desert, can convert goldmine to dunghill, can turn eagle to chick and hero and zero.

As a being, you carry the blood of your parents, and you may even suffer certain problems because you inherited it from your father. So, until you fight the evil blood you will continue to carry what is called the evil root of unknown curse.

Today, you need to disconnect yourself from unprofitable link.

1. All round stagnancy. Nothing works in business, career, ministry, marriage and other areas.

2. Broken marriages and relationships.

3. Diseases and infirmities.

4. Mistakes and errors. Take wrong steps leading to unpardonable mistakes.

5. Wrong positioning.

6. Wrong location.
    They ensure that you are at the wrong place and that you arrive at your place of blessing late so the blessing fly over your head.

7. Attracts hatred, rejection, and disappointment where there should be appointment.

8. Failure where there should be success. Especially failure at the edge of life changing breakthroughs.

9. Rising and falling.

10. Get and lose syndrome. This makes it impossible to retain good things.

11. Demotion where there should be promotion.

12. Cripples a person's life.

13. Amputates and diverts destinies.

14. Violent, tragic, or untimely death.

15. Profitless hard-work. This is because the person is laboring under a closed heaven.

Examples or signs of curses in one's life

In 1 King 16:34, a man woke up to help the city to build a wall that has collapsed for a long time. Suddenly, he lost his sons as a result of an unknown curse.

In the Jericho experience in 2 Kings 2:19; we learnt that not all that seems glamorous is good. In that place, the land was pleasant, but the water was bad and the land barren. Whatever link brings evil to your life, terminate that evil relationship today. Any association with evil friend, business, evil environment, evil house, evil church, evil movies or film, evil sons, and evil dressing is not good for you (1 Cor. 3:8) Evil communication, they say, corrupts good manner.

Thank God for Elisha whom God used to break the foundational curse upon Jericho. Elijah did not break it before he left. The man who issued the curse was Joshua. After the fall of Jericho wall, he said, "woe unto that man that will rebuild this city. When he is laying the foundation, his first son shall die and when he completes it, his last son shall die." Four hundred years later, it happened just like that. Now, they wanted the curse upon Jericho to be broken and Elisha broke it. I pray that every old curse that you are labouring under, shall be broken today in Jesus' name.

A man came into a city for trading and because that city was under a curse (Matt. 11:21 downwards), He became blind. It was when Jesus took him out of that city and touched him twice that he received his sight back and Jesus warned him not to return to the city so that more evil won't happen. This was because Jesus knew that prayers had stopped working in that city. Many today have many problems. This is because their sources have passed evil into their lives (read Mark 8:22-26).

As a being, you carry the blood of your parents, and you may even suffer certain problems because you inherited it from your father. So, until you fight the evil blood, you will continue to carry what is called the evil roots of unknown curse.

Today, you need to disconnect yourself from unprofitable links. You can't achieve this by fasting and prayer alone, but by your actions. It is in knowing when to say No to every and any unprofitable relationship. Abraham disconnected himself from Lot (Gen. 12:8-14); until Jonah was disconnected from the ship, the troubles never left them alone (Jonah 1:4-16). Matt. 13: In the parable of the sower, we learnt that some seeds were planted at the same time, yet some bore more fruit and others did not. The destiny of a seed depends on the ground it lands on.

May God relocate you from a stony ground to a fertile land today! If you sow a good seed where the soil is bad, it won't grow!

10 FACTS ABOUT CURSES

Curse can be cancelled

Curse can be diverted

Curse can be suspended

Curse can be transferred

Curse is contagious

Curse can be inherited

Curse can be prevented

Curse can be tranfer to another Isaiah 39:5-8.

Curse can be revise

One can be immunized against curse

DEALING WITH CURSES AND SPELLS

The destiny of man is a progressive one. However, certain forces arise to hinder the flow of progress in life. One of these forces is the unknown curse; this type of curse limits its victims.

To be limited is to be restricted, resisted and restrained.

It brings the spirit of limitation that delays destinies from getting to their ordained expected place; it makes people to perform below capacity and frustrates people from being all they should be.

The spirit of limitation produced by curses is a force that must be broken out from you if you must fulfil your destiny in a grand style.

If you don't break out of the bondage of curses, you can never get to where God has designed for you to get to and thereby, not enjoying all that has been prepared for your destiny.

There is nothing that limits or reduces man on earth as a curse and sin. They have been the major obstacles in the history of mankind. Curse and sin had reduced "the supernatural man" to an ordinary man. People like Samson, Saul, Gehaz, Judas and so on, have all been reduced from their glorious statuses by sin. Sin has killed much future potential, and as many that enjoy its pleasure. No one lives in sin and enjoys the benefits of dominion.

"Then lifted I up mine eyes, and saw, and behold four horns. And I said unto the angel that talked with me, What be these? And he answered me, These are the horns which have scattered Judah, Israel, and Jerusalem. And the Lord shewed me four carpenters. Then said I, What come these to do? And he spake, saying, These are the horns which have scattered Judah, so that no man did lift up his head: but these are come to fray them, to cast out the horns of the Gentiles, which lifted up their horn over the land of Judah to scatter it." (Zech. 1:18-21)

WHY SOME CURSE ARE DIFFICULT TO BREAK

Many of the Christians cannot command in the place of prayer because of many factors, some which are listed hereunder:

Hidden sin

Unsanctified mouth and tongue (Jer. 1:9-10; Song of Solomon 6:6-7)

Non-payment of tithe, vows and pledges (Job 22:27-28)

Not having good account with God (1Kings 17:1-2)

Not standing firm in God's presence. Jonah fled from God's presence (Jonah 1:3), but God called Abraham after 25 years that he had been following God and He said to him, "Walk before me and be thou perfect" (Gen. 17:1-27). Can you say you stand firm before God?

Ignorance

Fear

Because their spiritual battery is uncharged. Try to recharge your battery in prayer, fasting, Bible study, worship and fellowship with God.

You need higher power or corporate anointing. People chose Elisha because his anointing was comparable to that of Elijah. So, if a powerful native doctor puts a curse upon somebody, he or she would need a person with a higher anointing to break it.

HOW DO I BREAK FREE FROM CURSES AND EVIL COVENANTS?

Overcoming the forces of limitation does not depend on God alone. The responsibilities are laid on you and I. It is a matter of choice!

"For whatever is born of God overcomes the world. And this is the victory that has overcome the world; our faith". {1st John 5: 4-5}

Gen 23-24; Matt 7; 1 Chr. 5:1; Ezek. 18:2; Matt. 11:21-end

God does want us to be under this kind of thing.

Galatians 3:13 says, "Christ hath redeemed us from the curse of the law, being made a curse for us; for it is written, cursed is everyone that hangeth on a tree that the blessings of Abraham might come on the Gentiles through Jesus Christ." So, Jesus is our exchange. Matthew 18:18 says, "Whatsoever you bind on earth shall be bound in heaven, and whatsoever you loose on earth shall be loosed in heaven." 1 John 3:8 says, "For this purpose the Son of God was manifested that He might destroy the works of the devil."

Surrender your life to Jesus. You need His power to break evil curses. James 4:7.

Confess your sins and those of your ancestors.

Forgive yourself and others.
Renounce all attachment and involvement with curses.
Break all links and contacts with the enemy.
For example break evil soul ties and blood covenants properly and thoroughly.

Return all accursed properties or they will act as a ladder that keeps allowing the enemy back in. Satan will keep coming back so long as his property is in there.

Release yourself from all curses standing on your redemption through the blood of Jesus. Galatians 3:13-14, Colossians 2:14-15.

Replace curses with blessings.

Be obedient to God and His word.

Live a holy and righteous life to prevent reinforcement, regrouping, and counter attack.

Barricade you're your life with the blood of Jesus and the fire of God so that they not find their way back into your life and destiny.

SOMEONE'S LIFE CAN ALSO COME UNDER A CURSE IN THE FOLLOWING SITUATION.

GENERATIONAL CURSES

Lamentations 5:7: "Our fathers sinned, and are no more; it is we who have borne their iniquities."

Today, Christians lack huge knowledge and base everything on prayers, with Bible references to support their ignorance. It's very important we pray, but divine instructions and understanding spiritual laws can cause miraculous answers to prayers.

When Naaman came to Elisha, he instructed him to go and wash in the pool. This particular story is very important as it deals with generational issues. The reason why Elisha asked him to deep himself SEVEN times correlates to the fact that the disease had been in operation for seven generations. Each deep represents one generation and that was why he saw no effect until he got to the 7th deep. To ascertain these facts, when Gehazi misbehaved, Elisha's curse on him confirms the fact that this disease was a generational issue (Study the story carefully)

Exodus 34:7 says,

"Keeping mercy for thousands, forgiving iniquity and transgression and sin, and that will by no means clear the guilty; visiting (punishing) the iniquity of the fathers upon the children, and upon the children's children, unto the third and to the fourth generation."

Psalm 11:3 says, "If the foundations be destroyed, what can the righteous do?"

Note: The word "righteous". Sadly, with a little effort, scriptural verses can be found that will 'prove' any and all points of view, provided one removes all the surrounding text which actually determines its meaning.

I have seen with my eyes, deliverances where demons burst out of anger, querying the minister if he was there when the fathers dedicated them to him. Demons understand their rights very well, even as angels do.

Demons are behind every idol worshipped, and so, Satan has the spiritual rights to afflict a Christian with a faulty foundation.

Almost every family has a hidden spiritual constitution that controls its lineage from generation to generation, kept by the evil spirit called principality of household, demonic caretaker or strong man. These evil powers have been standing as spiritual gateman. E. g. If any member of the family is coming from payer house, they will withhold their blessing and say nobody in your family must pass this boundary. They use the image of your family to fight you in your dream, feed you and curse you to have sex in your dream, in order for you to lose your miracle, just because your fore-fathers had covenanted with them in the past, seeking power or protection

So many parents have set standards for their children and these evil standards must be broken i. e. if your parent didn't build any house, you must break the standard because there is the possibility that you won't build a house if care is not taken. Also, if your mother had delayed child bearing, this may affect your life.

I pray today, the entire evil standard laid down by your parents will not be your portion in Jesus' name.

 Say this prayer:

Father, disconnect me from the frequency of my father or my parents.

Many have problems today that may be traced to their parents.

In the Bible, the same problem happened to our father, Abraham and it reoccurred to Isaac, his son. However, thank God for the life of Jacob who broke the evil standard (Read Gen 20:1 - 2; Gen 26: 1- 9; Jer. 35:1-14).

The Rechabites had an evil ancestral standard that none of the children could build a house. That will not be our potion in Jesus' name. If nobody ever travelled or graduated or even have a good job in your family, as a person, you must break such a standard.

If God says you shall lend to nations, can you do it in your present situation? (Deut. 28:12–13).

You need to plan big and think big, so that you can get a big report (Prov 23: 8). From today, you shall set a new standard for your generation. Remember, nobody celebrates a failure, but an achiever will always be celebrated.

Stop condemning yourself over your poor background or your parent's lack of education. It is not a problem to be born poor; the problem is to die poor.

Moses was born and worse still, a slave. He was born during the time a decree was made that a male child must not be given birth to, but the same house that made that evil decision took up the responsibilities of Moses' upbringing. Moses broke the standards of slavery. The world is waiting for you!

In Jesse`s family, nobody ever went to the palace or became king, but David broke the record; that today, people still believe that David was the first king of Israel, but he wasn't. He only broke the standards. What standard must you break?

Some generational curses can show themselves through health issues or bad habits. Some families struggle with alcoholism, womanizing, lies, criminal records, cancer, diabetes, high BP and these things can also be evident in the life of the children. Sometimes, we give them medical explanation as hereditary issues. What of cases of 2-4 people being mad in a family? Is madness hereditary?

The Israelites had to suffer affliction for 400 years; why? It could be that Exodus 34:7 was at work since a generation is 100 years and this could mean that somehow, along the line, their fathers may have transgressed against God. Remember, Abraham's father named "Terah" was an idol worshipper.

Genesis 15:13:

The Lord tells Abraham, "Know for certain that your offspring will be sojourners in a land that is not theirs and will be servants there, and they will be afflicted for four hundred years." God knows everything that will happen, and He revealed part of the future to Abraham.

Curses of disobedience; dishonouring one's parents: The reason why so many people are cursed is because they dishonour their parents. It is not possible for anybody with wrong attitudes towards his or her parents to come under the full blessing of the Lord. The Bible says, "Honour your father and your mother that your days may be long upon the land which the Lord thy God giveth thee." This is the first commandment with a promise (Ephesians 6:2-3). Dishonouring parents puts a person under God's curse.

Sexual perversion: Adultery, fornication or incest puts a person under a curse.

Injustice to the meek or the helpless: Exploiting your neighbour's weakness(es), stealing money from the blind, telling lies to somebody who is not educated, so that you can extract money from him, abusing a person in a language he does not understand, procuring abortion, etc can put a person automatically under God's curse.

Hatred for people of God: There are people who hate the Jews and always speak against them. Such people place themselves under a curse because the Bible says, "Abraham, anyone who curses your children shall be cursed, anyone who blesses them shall be blessed." If somebody hates the Jews, he automatically comes under God's curse.

Stealing and cursing: Zechariah 5:1-3 says, "Then I turned, and lifted up mine eyes, and looked, and behold a flying roll. And he said unto me, what seest thou? And I answered, I see a flying roll ; the length thereof is twenty cubits and the breadth thereof ten cubits. Then said he unto me, this is the curse that goeth forth over the face of the whole earth; for everyone that stealeth shall be cut off as on this side according to it; and every one that sweareth shall be cut off as on that side according to it." So, stealing and cursing puts a person under God's curse. Somebody takes something and swears under oath that he did not take it, such a person automatically comes under God's curse. Somebody goes to the court and swears to tell the truth and nothing but the truth, but his next sentence is a lie. Such a person automatically comes under a curse. That is what the Bible says. Such people need to repent. Repentance is the answer.

Cursed be the man that trusted in man: Jeremiah 17:5-6 tells us why another type of curse can come upon people. It says, "Thus saith the Lord, cursed be the man that trusteth in man and maketh flesh his arm and whose heart departeth from the Lord. For he shall be like the heath in the desert and shall not see when good cometh but shall inhabit the parched places in the wilderness, in a salt land and not inhabited." Trusting in man or yourself, your natural ability, cleverness or education, instead of depending on God, brings one under the curse of God.

Tithelessness: Malachi 3:8-9 tells us about another curse. It is about being stingy with God. The passage says, "Will a man rob God? Yet ye have robbed me. But ye say, wherein have we robbed thee? In tithes and offerings. Ye are cursed with a curse: for ye have robbed me, even this whole nation."

Failure in tithes and offerings is a strong key to poverty. When you give God your tithes and offerings, don't sit down like a businessman who said, "O' God, I have just paid ten thousand naira to you and that means that you have to give me hundred thousand back. God, do you understand?" In this case, you are doing business, you are not giving. It must be willingly and cheerfully given. Believers don't borrow their tithes. If you borrow your tithe, you must pay twenty per cent on top by the time that you are bringing it back. Ten per cent is just the minimum that God wants you to bring to His house. It is different from the offerings which you must give to God. Failure to do that would amount to God not opening to you the windows of heaven and pouring out to you a blessing. Many believers are labouring under this curse without knowing. They always say, "I pray all the prayer points, I did all the things that should be done and yet nothing."

The question is, are you faithful in paying your tithe?

Anyone who wants to be cursed should be stingy with God. But the person that wants to be blessed should be generous with God. When people do the work of God miserably, they pronounce curses on themselves.

If you have come under any of them, repentance is the only solution. No prayer can help you out. Any prophet that says he can help you is lying. You must repent.

CURSES FROM THE AGGRIEVED: Curses from fellow men. Some people are under curses by their parents, husbands or wives. A teacher may also curse a pupil in the school. All these things would be binding because those who issued them have authority over those they cursed. The Bible says that the husband is the head of the home. If you are a woman and you do not really agree with that, it does not matter because the word of the Bible is final. If God says the husband is the head and the husband issues a curse on his wife, it could be binding on that wife until she loosens herself. Likewise, if parents issue curses on their children, it could come to pass.

Proverbs 28: 9: "He that turneth away his ears from learning the law, even his prayer shall be abomination." So, a person's prayer can become an abomination. It means that when those who do not have God in their lives, who are not born again, start to pray, they are indirectly cursing themselves.

SELF-INFLICTED CURSE: Self-imposed curses: What you say about yourself will come back to you. These are curses people put on themselves every day. When somebody says, "I wish I were dead." What is the good in living? The whole of life is a big bag of frustrations, or he says, "I am always having bad luck, I don't have any friend," the person is cursing himself and it is binding. A lot of people do that every day; they commit spiritual murder with their mouth.

Cursed herbalists and diviners: Another form of horizontal curses are those from some people representing the devil. Herbalists and diviners that claim to be able to see things belong to this group. Sometimes, it is when you accept the vision that they see that it happens. They are cursed indirectly. If somebody says, "I see a vision that you will marry four husbands or you will have accident or you will lose your money," and you do not reject it immediately, it will become binding. You must reject such things straight away.

Sin is the fastest killer of any vision and destiny.

It doesn't matter who commits it. John Wycliffe said,

"Sin is nothing, and men when they sinned become nothing. If then, sinners are nothing, it is evident that they can possess nothing."

 Stinginess: Proverbs 11: 24 says, "There is that scattereth, and yet increaseth; and there is that withholdeth more than is meet, but it tendeth to poverty." Stinginess leads to poverty. This is where God's mathematics is different from our own mathematics. It is more logical to keep money, hoard it, or pile it up to become rich. But God's law says that he that scatters increases, but he that withholds, gets poorer.

A certain man was on a salary of five hundred naira and was paying fifty naira as tithe per month. After some time, God blessed him and he started earning five thousand naira per month and as such, he had to pay five hundred naira for tithe every month. This man went to the pastor and said he needed counselling. The pastor asked him why he needed counselling and he said that five hundred naira was too much for him to pay as tithe every month because he felt that it could buy so many things. The pastor said, "No problem sir, let me pray that God should return you to your former income, so that you will be able to pay fifty naira which you can afford."

A lot of Christians treat God as if He is an errand boy who they give tips. God is not also a beggar. He does not need your alms. If you are reading this message and you are still stingy, stop it because the Bible says that a stingy person is cursed. The key to receiving is giving. Anyone who does not give is like the Dead Sea. The problem of the Dead Sea is that it does not give out, it keeps everything inside and so, it stinks because it is not refreshed.

 Not contributing to God's work: Haggai 1: 6-8 says, "You have sown much, and bring in little; ye eat, but ye have not enough; ye drink, but ye are not filled with drink; ye clothe you, but there is none warm; and he that earneth wages earneth wages to put it into a bag with holes. Thus saith the Lord of hosts; Consider your ways. Go up to the mountain, and bring wood, and build the house; and I will take pleasure in it, and I will be glorified, saith the Lord."

Anytime there is something to be done in the Church and pledges are taken, please don't be left out, even if it is only ten kobo that you can afford. Put something down for the Lord for He sees your heart, provided you have done according to your ability. Not contributing to the Lord's work is like watching your father's business go down and you feel unconcerned about it. It is this attitude that makes foolish Christian leaders to print harvest pamphlets and envelopes and distribute them to lodge members because they want money. The harvest that Jesus was talking about was the harvest of souls, not the harvest of yam and plantain and bazaar which is really fraudulent in the house of God. It is wrong to put down a tuber of yam that someone bought for ten naira and to start ringing bell for someone to buy it for more.

Giving to God in small measures: God measures your giving by the amount you have for yourself and not by the amount you give. Jesus said that that widow contributed more than everybody did because she put all that she had. It is a pleasure when God gives you something and you are able to give it back to Him. Luke 6: 38 says, "Give, and it shall be given unto you; good measure, pressed down, and shaken together, and running over, shall men give into your bosom. For with the same measure that ye mete withal it shall be measured to you again."

Engaging in the wrong business: Luke 5: 4 - 6 says, "Now when he had left speaking, he said unto Simon, Launch out into the deep, and let down your nets for a draught. And Simon answering said unto him, Master, we have toiled all night, and have taken nothing; nevertheless, at thy word I will let down the net. And when they had this done, they inclosed a great multitude of fishes: and their net broke..." The man who has prosperity was there, and when Peter failed, he told him what to do. When Peter saw what Jesus did, he was astonished, and those who were with him. In verse 10, Jesus said unto Simon, "Fear not; from henceforth thou shall catch men." This means that Peter was supposed to be catching men, but he was busy catching fish and was not successful. Even when Jesus died, he went back to fishing and still did not catch anything (John 21: 3-6).

Not caring for ministers of God: Mathew 10: 41 says, "He that receiveth a prophet shall receive a prophet's reward; and he that receiveth a righteous man in the name of a righteous man shall receive a righteous man's reward." Ministers of God are not meant to be begging people for money. They are not supposed to be commercial ministers like it is these days. But the Church of God is meant to look after its ministers.

Not giving to the poor: Proverbs 28: 27 says, "He that giveth unto the poor shall not lack: but he that hideth his eyes shall have many a curse." Giving to the poor helps you to have abundance.

Pride: Some people feel that they are too big to do some jobs whereas, they have no job. They would say, "This is not the kind of job for university graduates. I cannot do it." They then begin to walk about the street, jobless. They always forget that God takes a little thing and then multiplies it. This is why rich illiterate men employ many university graduates today; yet they do not want to do the kind of jobs that those illiterate men did before they became rich. They feel that they are too big to begin business in a little dirty way. God will deliver all those who have the spirit of pride in them in Jesus' name.

Ostentatious living: Some people like showing off. As soon as they collect their salary, the people they bought things from would be waiting to collect their money. They want to look better than everybody does and so, they keep paying debts.

Engaging in secret sins: Sin hinders blessings; they stop God from working. As a believer, if you have some sins that you are committing secretly, you have the key of poverty in your hands.

Demonic activities: The major factors responsible for the poverty of black people in this environment are demonic activities.

Curses from the powerless because of injustice: Curses can arise where there is deep abiding injustice against an ethnic group. Saul's blood thirsty massacre of the Gibeonites which lay uncorrected for years later resulted in a curse and a famine in the time of David.

(2 Samuel 21:1 NKJV) Now, there was a famine in the days of David for three years, year after year; and David inquired of the LORD. And the LORD answered, "It is because of Saul and his blood thirsty house, because he killed the Gibeonites."

David broke this curse by going back to the offended ethnic group, humbly asking how they would like to see justice done and then enacting it. After ten of Saul's sons were hung, the famine ended (2 Samuel 21:1-14).

Slackness in ministry can result in a curse: The priests in Malachi were under a curse because of their slackness in God's work (Malachi 2:2) and Prophet Jeremiah cries out "cursed be he who is slack in doing the Lord's work (Jeremiah 48:10). If you are in ministry, do the work of the Lord diligently and obey His specific instructions if you have been given such instructions.

Returned curses:

Examples of returned curses are;

When you curse somebody higher than you, it returns back (Ecclesiastes 10:20).

When you lost your property and place curse, letter discover it and still use it, the curse will return. Judges 17:1-end

Curses from evil altar:

In Numbers 23, Balaam raised altars in an attempt to curse Israel.

The altar of Baal in Gideon's family which Gideon destroyed (Judges 6:25-32).

Prophetic curses; why do enemies curse:

Goliath's curses against David were "by his gods" (1 Samuel 17:43) and were ineffective for reasons we shall see later. The David-and-Goliath encounter was a power encounter of one spiritual system against the other and both contenders came in the name of their respective deities. Shamans and magicians such as Balaam were hired to curse people in Numbers 23. To curse the people of God, so that they will make mistakes, sin, disconnect from their God, be sick, fight themselves and confused in order to make enemies win the battle.

Curse of breaking covenants

Revelation 22:18-19

Unspoken curse: when you are misleading blinds and strangers (Deuteronomy 27:14-26). CURSE OF GOD: This is where people violate his word.

Proverbs 3:33: The curse of the LORD is in the house of the wicked: but he blesseth the habitation of the just.

CURSE OF MAN: When someone has lawful authority over you, such as a parent has over a child.

Matthew 15:4: For God commanded, saying, Honour thy father and mother: and, He that curseth father or mother, let him die the death.

Romans 13:1-2: Let everyone be subject to the governing authorities, for there is no authority except that which God has established. The authorities that exist have been established by God. 2 Consequently, whoever rebels against the authority is rebelling against what God has instituted, and those who do so will bring judgment on themselves.

CURSE OF SOWING AND REAPING: What you did in the past will come back to you.

CURSE OF THE PROPHETS: Psalm 105:14-15: He allowed no one to oppress them; He rebuked kings on their behalf: "Do not touch my anointed ones, (B) or harm my prophets."

CURSE OF THE ACCURSED: Bringing an accursed object in your home, being around someone cursed or living in a cursed community, you bring a curse against yourself. Joshua 1:7: Only be thou strong and very courageous that thou mayest observe to do according to all the law which Moses my servant commanded thee: turn not from it to the right hand or to the left, that thou mayest prosper withersoever thou goest.

GENERATIONAL/INHERITED CURSE: Exodus 20:5: You shall not bow down to them or worship them; for I, the LORD your God, am a jealous God, punishing the children for the sin of the parents to the third and fourth generation of those who hate me,

CURSE OF UNFORGIVENESS: Failing to forgive others or being bitter toward others will bring a curse upon you and hinder your spiritual relationship with God. Hebrews 12;14-15: Make every effort to live in peace with everyone and to be holy; without holiness no one will see the Lord. 15 See to it that no one falls short of the grace of God and that no bitter root grows up to cause trouble and defile many. Curse of the Law: When God's law is broken and the only way to get out is to repent and obey God.

CURSE OF SATAN: The simplest of all the curses and once you have established a relationship with Jesus and have decided to follow Him, Satan can't bother you. These curses aren't to scare you, but to identify problems in your life in order to help you make a better life. Instead of inflicting curses upon yourself, why not inflict a blessing?

BIBLICAL CAUSES FOR CURSES

Curses from Disobedience and Sin

Curses are the results of disobedience either from self or through the family line. In the Bible we can see sickness, pestilence, blindness, madness. It is an expression of the universal law of sowing and reaping. We reap in areas of disobedience. If we are experiencing failure, we look to see where we or someone in our line has broken God's covenants. (Deut 28 and Deut 28:15)

Curses from Self-Centered Life

A self-centered life leads to curses. (Deut 27:16-26) ☐ Peace and rest is found in fulfilling the purposes of God. If we don't find out purpose, peace will fee from us.   (Jere 48:10) ☐ Associating with those who are breaking God's laws or who are cursed is equal to fellowshipping with a covenant breaker, (Josh 7:1) and plagues are upon those who do not separate from covenant breakers.   (Rev 18:1-5) ☐ We are subject to the authority of God and when we revile authority, we bring condemnation upon ourselves. (Rom 13:1)

Word Curses

 There are spoken curses from others that can hold power over us: (Prov 18:31, Isaiah 65, James 3:911, Prov 11:9) ☐ God will bless those who bless us, and curse those that curse us. (Gen 12:3) ☐ If someone curses a Christian, the very curse they plead will return on them. (Gen 12:3, Ps 109:17-19, Romans 12) ☐ There are self-imposed curses on us when we speak or agree with words spoken over us that do not agree with what God has spoken over us. (Gen 27:13 Matt 27:45) Some people would even label these as "vows". "I will never get it right". ☐ We can speak over others - blessing or curses. (Prov 26:2 1 Peter 3:9)

Curses from Generation Sin

There are negative effects of generational sin. ☐ Eve's rebellion led to pain in childbirth. (Gen

3:16) ☐ Abraham lied, Jacob lied. (Gen 20:2, 27:7) ☐ Generational curses can affect a nation. (Is 24) ☐ Curses can affect increase "You sow a wind and reap a whirlwind. (Hosea 8:7) ☐ Children suffer from the sins of their fathers. (II Sam 12:1-19) ☐ Also see: Deut 5:9 23:2,3 38:45,46, 58,59; Num 14:18; Lev 26:40-42; Ex 25:3,4 34:67; Isaiah 65:6,7; Dan 9:16; Matt 2:7:25; John 9:1-2

LOCATION OR ASSOCIATION CURSE

2 Kings 2:19-22

And the men of the city said unto Elisha, Behold, I pray thee, the situation of this city is pleasant, as my lord seeth: but the water is naught, and the ground barren. And he said, Bring me a new cruse, and put salt therein. And they brought it to him. And he went forth unto the spring of the waters, and cast the salt in there, and said, Thus saith the Lord, I have healed these waters; there shall not be from thence any more death or barren land. So the waters were healed unto this day, according to the saying of Elisha which he spake

Joshua 6:26

And Joshua adjured them at that time, saying, Cursed be the man before the Lord, that riseth up and buildeth this city Jericho: he shall lay the foundation thereof in his firstborn, and in his youngest son shall he set up the gates of it

1 Kings 16:34-35

In his days did Hiel the Bethelite build Jericho: he laid the foundation thereof in Abiram his firstborn, and set up the gates thereof in his youngest son Segub, according to the word of the Lord, which he spake by Joshua the son of Nun.

Capernaum (Mark 8:22)

And he cometh to Bethsaida; and they bring a blind man unto him, and besought him to touch him. And he took the blind man by the hand, and led him out of the town; and when he had spit on his eyes, and put his hands upon him, he asked him if he saw ought. And he looked up, and said, I see men as trees, walking. After that he put his hands again upon his eyes, and made him look up: and he was restored, and saw every man clearly. And he sent him away to his house, saying, Neither go into the town, nor tell it to any in the town.

Matthew 11:20-24

Then began he to upbraid the cities wherein most of his mighty works were done, because they repented not: Woe unto thee, Chorazin! woe unto thee, Bethsaida! for if the mighty works, which were done in you, had been done in Tyre and Sidon, they would have repented long ago in sackcloth and ashes. But I say unto you, It shall be more tolerable for Tyre and Sidon at the day of judgment, than for you. And thou, Capernaum, which art exalted unto heaven, shalt be brought down to hell: for if the mighty works, which have been done in thee, had been done in Sodom, it would have remained until this day. But I say unto you, That it shall be more tolerable for the land of Sodom in the day of judgment, than for thee.

HOW DO CURSES COME INTO A PERSON'S LIFE?

Someone's life can also come under a curse in the following situation.

You can come under a curse under the following circumstances:

Disobedient to God and His word. For example Adam. Genesis 3:17-19.

Failure to do restitution when it is required by the word of God. For example failure   to return stolen properties such as stolen spouses, properties   from   sugar   daddies   and
 mummies.

Bloodshed particularly of innocent blood.

Breaking covenants such as marriage vows.

Cures from evil altar

Curse of breaking covenants

Curse of the powerless

Curses from the aggrieved

Dishonoring of one's parents.

Engagement in sexual perversion

Engaging in sex outside of marriage. Breaking marriage vows.

Evil association curses

Failure to restitute when it is required by the word of God. For example, failure to return stolen properties such as stolen spouses, properties from sugar daddies and mummies.

Generational curse

Guilty of bloodshed.

Hidden/unknown curses (Capernaum. Mark 8:22-)

How do I break free from curses?

How to prevent curses

Idolatry.

Location or association curse

Oppression of the helpless. Isaiah 58:6-8, Ezekiel 22:29.

Possessing accursed things.

Prophetic cures

Put trust in men instead of God.

Release from curses attached to evil covenants

Returned curses

Sex outside of marriage.

Sexual perversion cures

Speaking evil of men of God. Allow God to judge them.

Speaking evil of the men of God. Allow God to judge them.

Strongholds of curses (why some curses are difficult to break)

Take back whatever they have stolen from you.

The curseless personalities

Through inheritance.

Through polygamy.

Trusting in men instead of God.

Unspoken curses

When you appropriate God's glory for yourself. God is a jealous God and will not share His glory with anyone.

When you appropriate God's glory for yourself. God is jealous God and will not   share His glory with anyone.

You have cursed things in your possession.

You have to break all the blood covenants involved.

You have to break all the evil soul ties involved –
write down all the names and pray your way
through.

Genesis 49:1-29

And Jacob called unto his sons, and said: Gather
yourselves together, that I may tell you that
which shall befall you in the last days.

Gather yourselves together, and hear, ye sons of
Jacob; and hearken unto Israel, your father.

Reuben, thou art my firstborn, my might, and the
beginning of my strength, the excellency of
dignity, and the excellency of power:

Unstable as water, thou shalt not excel; because
thou wentest up to thy father's bed; then
defiledst thou it: he went up to my couch.

Lamentations 5:1-22

Deuteronomy 28:15-68:

Possessing accursed things. (Genesis 31:32)

Cures from disobedient; dishonoring one's parents: Ephesians 6:2-3

Cures from evil altar Numbers 23 Balaam raised altars (Judges 6:25-32).

Cures from the enemies; Goliath's curses against David were "by his gods" (1 Samuel 17:43)

Curse of breaking covenants Revelation 22:18-19

Cursed be the man that trusted in man; Jeremiah 17:5-6

Cursed Herbalists and diviners: Demonic agents. The major factors responsible for the poverty of black people in this environment are demonic activities.

Disobedience to God and His word. (Adam – Genesis 3:17-19).

Engaging in secret sins: Sin hinders blessings. They stop God from working. As a believer, if you have some sins that you are committing secretly, you have the key of poverty in your hands.

Engaging in sex outside of marriage. Breaking marriage vows.

Engaging in the wrong business: Luke 5: 4 – 6 John 21: 3-6.

Failure in tithes and offerings is a strong key to poverty. Malachi 3:8-9

Failure to restitute when it is required by the word of God. For example, failure to return stolen properties such as stolen spouses, properties from sugar daddies and mummies.

Giving to God in small measures: Luke 6: 38

Guilty of bloodshed.

Hatred for people of God: cursed is anyone that cursed

Hiding or unknown curse. (Capernaum.   Mark 8:22-)

Idolatry.

Inherited or generational curse. 11 king 5:27, 11 Samuel 3:28-29

Injustice to the meek or the helpless: . Some people are under curses by their parents, husbands or wives. A teacher may also curse a pupil in the school.

Location or association curse: Curse on Jericho Joshua 6:26. 1 kings 16:34-35. 2 kings 2:19-22. Curse on Capernaum. Matthew 11:20-24. Mark 8:22-26.

Not caring for ministers of God: Mathew 10: 41

Oppressing the helpless. Isaiah 58:6-8, Ezekiel 22:29.

Prophetic cures. Jeremiah 22:29-30.

Returned curse. Ecclesiastes 10:20

Rivalry and Opposition curses can come through opposition Number 22:6

Self-imposed curses. False swearing

cures from engagement in Sexual pervasion; when you rape a lady or you denied that you are not the one responsible for her pregnancy

Speaking evil of the men of God. Allow God to judge them. (Genesis 27:29)

Stealing and cursing: Zechariah 5:1-3

Stinginess: Proverbs 11: 24. to the poor: Proverbs 28: 27. to the work of the Lord: Haggai 1:6-8

Unspoken curse; (Cures from grief one) when you are misleading blinds and strangers, Deuteronomy 27:14-26.

When you appropriate God's glory for yourself. God is a jealous God and will not share His glory with anyone.

You can marry into curse Hosea 9:14

Check out the jealous nature of God and His glory in

Deuteronomy 27:14-26.

14. And the Levites shall speak, and say unto all the men of Israel with a loud voice,

15. Cursed be the man that maketh any graven or molten image, an abomination unto the LORD, the work of the hands of the craftsman, and putteth it in a secret place. And all the people shall answer and say, Amen.

16. Cursed be he that setteth light by his father or his mother. And all the people shall say, Amen.

17. Cursed be he that removeth his neighbour's landmark. And all the people shall say, Amen.

18. Cursed be he that maketh the blind to wander out of the way. And all the people shall say, Amen.

19. Cursed be he that perverteth the judgment of the stranger, fatherless, and widow. And all the people shall say, Amen.

20. Cursed be he that lieth with his father's wife; because he uncovereth his father's skirt. And all the people shall say, Amen.

21. Cursed be he that lieth with any manner of beast. And all the people shall say, Amen.

22. Cursed be he that lieth with his sister, the daughter of his father, or the daughter of his mother. And all the people shall say, Amen.

23. Cursed be he that lieth with his mother-in-law. And all the people shall say, Amen.

24. Cursed be he that smiteth his neighbour secretly. And all the people shall say, Amen.

25. Cursed be he that taketh reward to slay an innocent person. And all the people shall say, Amen.

26. Cursed be he that confirmeth not all the words of this law to do them. And all the people shall say, Amen.

These passages tell us twelve categories of a curse. If a curse is working in our life, it will always have a cause. Proverbs 26:2 says

'Like a sparrow in its flitting and a swallow in its flying so a curse without a cause CANNOT alight.'

These are the horns which have scattered Judah, so that no man did lift up his head..

Zech 1:18-21

"And if a soul sin, and commit any of these things which are forbidden to be done by the commandments of the Lord; though he wist it not, yet is he guilty, and shall bear his iniquity." Lev 5:17

"Hear, O earth: behold, I will bring evil upon this people, even the fruit of their thoughts, because they have not hearkened unto my words, nor to my law, but rejected it. Jer 6:19

CATEGORIES AND TYPES OF CURES:

Curses from Disobedience and Sin

Curses are the results of disobedience either from self or through the family line. In the Bible we can see sickness, pestilence, blindness, madness. It is an expression of the universal law of sowing and reaping. We reap in areas of disobedience. If we are experiencing failure, we look to see where we or someone in our line has broken God's covenants. (Duet 28 and Duet 28:15)

Curses from Self-Centered Life

A self-centered life leads to curses. (Deut 27:16-26) Peace and rest is found in fulfilling the purposes of God. If we don't find out purpose, peace will fee from us. (Jere 48:10) Associating with those who are breaking God's laws or who are cursed is equal to fellowshipping with a covenant breaker, (Josh 7:1) and plagues are upon those who do not separate from covenant breakers. (Rev 18:1-5) We are subject to the authority of God and when we revile authority, we bring condemnation upon ourselves. (Rom 13:1)

Word Curses

There are spoken curses from others that can hold power over us: (Prov 18:31, Isaiah 65, James 3:911, Prov 11:9) God will bless those who bless us, and curse those that curse us. (Gen 12:3) If someone curses a Christian, the very curse they plead will return on them. (Gen 12:3, Ps 109:17-19, Romans 12) There are self-imposed curses on us when we speak or agree with words spoken over us that do not agree with what God has spoken over us. (Gen 27:13 Matt 27:45) Some people would even label these as "vows". "I will never get it right". ☐ We can speak over others - blessing or curses. (Prov 26:2 1 Peter 3:9)

Slackness in ministry can result in a curse: Doing God's work with deception The priests in Malachi were under a curse because of their slackness in God's work (Malachi 2:2) and the prophet Jeremiah cries out "cursed be he who is slack in doing the Lord's work (Jeremiah 48:10).

Idolatry: Serving and worshipping false gods, occult involvement, special baths in the sea, etc. could place a person under a curse. A person whose ancestors were involved in these things also comes under the curse even though he did not do so himself. Out of their activities some forefathers put their descendants under a curse. Until anyone concerned releases himself from the curse and breaks it, he will not be free. Idolatry or involvement in occult practices puts one under automatic curse. There is no prayer that can help such a person except he repents.

Curse of the powerless and grief fellow; Curses from the powerless because of the injustice; curse can alight where there is deep abiding injustice against an ethnic group. Saul's bloodthirsty massacre of the Gibeonites, which lay uncorrected for years, later resulted in a curse and a famine in the time of David.(2 Samuel 21:1 NKJV) Now there was a famine in the days of David for three years, year after year; and David inquired of the LORD. And the LORD answered, "It is because of Saul and his bloodthirsty house, because he killed the Gibeonites."

David broke this curse by going back to the offended ethnic group, humbly asking how they would like to see justice done and then enacting it. After ten of Saul's sons were hung the famine ended. (2 Samuel 21:1-14).

Exodus 34:7 says,

"Keeping mercy for thousands, forgiving iniquity and transgression and sin, and that will by no means clear the guilty; visiting (punishing) the iniquity of the fathers upon the children, and upon the children's children, unto the third and to the fourth generation."

Psalm 11:3 says, "If the foundations be destroyed, what can the righteous do?"

Almost every family has a hidden spiritual constitution that controls its lineage from generation to generation, kept by the evil spirit called principality of household, demonic caretaker or strong man. These evil powers have been standing as spiritual gatemen. For instance, if any member of the family is coming from the prayer house, they will withhold their blessing and say nobody in your family must pass this boundary. They use the image of your family to fight you in your dream, feed you and curse you to have sex in your dream, in order for you to lose your miracle, just because your fore-fathers had covenanted with them while seeking power and protection

So many parents have set standards for their children and these evil standards must be broken i.e. if your parents didn't build any house, you must break the standard because there is the possibility that you won't build a house if care is not taken. If your mother had a delay in childbearing, this may affect your life.

Many have problems today that may be traced to their parents. In the Bible, the same problem happened to our ancestors, Abraham, and it reoccurred to Isaac, his son. However, thank God for the life of Jacob who broke the evil standard (Read Gen 20:1 - 2; Gen 26: 1- 9; Jer. 35:1-14).

The Rechabites had an evil ancestral standard that none of the children could build a house. That will not be our portion in Jesus' name. If nobody ever traveled or graduated or even have a good job in your family, as a person, you must break such a standard. If God says you shall lend to nations, can you do it in your present situation? (Deut. 28:12–13).

You need to plan big and think big so that you can get a big report (Prov. 23: 8). From today, you shall set a new standard for your generation. Remember, nobody celebrates a failure, but an achiever. Stop condemning yourself over your poor background or your parent's lack of education. It is not a problem to be born poor; the problem is to die poor.

Moses was born and worse still, a slave. He was born during the time a decree was made that a male child must not be given birth to, but the same house that made that evil decision took up the responsibilities of Moses' upbringing. Moses broke the standards of slavery. The world is waiting for you!

In Jesse`s family, nobody ever went to the palace or became king, but David broke the record; that today, people still believe that David was the first king of Israel, but he wasn't. He only broke the standards. What standard must you break?

Some generational curses can show themselves through health issues or bad habits. Some families struggle with alcoholism, womanizing, lies, crimes, cancer, diabetes, high BP and the likes, with the evidence in the life of their children. Sometimes, we give them a medical explanation as hereditary issues. What of cases of 2 to 4 people being mad in a family? Is madness hereditary?

The Israelites had to suffer affliction for 400 years; why? It could be that Exodus 34:7 was at work and this could mean that somehow, along the line, their fathers may have transgressed against God. Remember, Abraham's father, Terah was an idol worshipper.

Genesis 15:13:

The Lord tells Abraham, "Know for certain that your offspring will be sojourners in a land that is not theirs and will be servants there, and they will be afflicted for four hundred years."

God knows everything that will happen, and He revealed part of the future to Abraham.

Curses are the results of disobedience either from self or through the family line. In the Bible, we can see sickness, pestilence, blindness, madness. It is an expression of the universal law of sowing and reaping. We reap in areas of disobedience. If we are experiencing failure, we look to see where we or someone in our line has broken God's covenants. (Deut 28 and Deut 28:15)

When a person does the work of God deceitfully, he gets to be cursed as placed by God. The solution to such will be to refrain from doing God's work deceitfully. (Jer.48:10)

Associating with those who are breaking God's laws or who are cursed is equal to fellowshipping with a covenant breaker, (Josh 7:1) and plagues are upon those who do not separate from covenant breakers. (Rev 18:1-5) We are subject to the authority of God and when we revile authority, we bring condemnation upon ourselves. (Rom 13:1)

Some locations sometimes might be cursed that those who dwell there begin to feel the effect of the curse. The references below drawn from the scripture prove the truth that a place or location can be accursed, but thanks to God who is able to heal the land.

MYSTERY AND THE EFFECT OF CURSES

The ignorance of curse does not disturb the work. It even makes it more dangerous, but if you know that there is a curse upon you, you can quickly pray and fast about it. However, can you pray for what you don't know of?

No man will be justified for being ignorant, for ignorance is not an excuse. Ignorance is an agent of death which can cut one's life short. The problem many people have today is lack of knowledge; Hosea 4: 6. They don't know what to do, how to do it, and when to do it, and as a result of this, they are living a stagnant life.

A curse is a tragedy that moves from generation to generation. You have to understand that. This is why we have a lot of educated illiterates around. Their chains of degrees cannot help them. Education is not an ability to nullify curses or the ability to defeat the forces limiting your life.

A family or a community can be in a position where it never produces a great person. There are communities where you cannot find any educated man.

A family weakness can move from generation to generation. In some families, it is the curse of premature death. God said to Eli that no man in his family would enter his grave with grey hair. There are families like that. There are some families where their members never rise above a particular level. In Joshua 9:23 we see the curse that was put upon a whole tribe. It says, "Now therefore ye are cursed, and there shall none of you be freed from being bondmen, and hewers of wood and drawers of water for the house of my God."

Being cursed is a terrible thing in one's life i.e. if a curse or sanction is placed on a student; no matter how brilliant he/she may be he/she will not pass the exam. Many houses are under curses and nobody is ever willing to rent them. Many single brothers and sisters are under spells and sanctions to an extent that nobody approaches them for a relationship. Many marriages are barren because it is under a spell or curse. Hosea 9:14.

Curses are real and in some cases they are even lethal; Ezekiel talks of magic charms that hunted lives (Ezekiel 13:18-20). Curses are on the rise in Western culture as people dabble more and more in the occult and in organizations where people take secret oaths that invoke curses (such as the Masons, ORF, Ogboni, Lorge. Etc.). Emotionally curses produce deep confusion and despair and an inability to think straight.

Escape by physical relocation is not the answer but spiritual relocation; Physical relocation does not stop a curse, exept it is locational curse like mark 8:22-.

Daniel 10:1-3&10-13. Daniel prayed, answers were released but at the second heaven, there was a confrontation by a particular power

Every country has a rulling and controlling power over it, Every city has a rulling and controlling power over it, No matter how advanced it is, how civilised it claims to be, there is a power controlling it, Every throne has a spiritual throne, Every government has a spiritual government cabinet, Every location has it's characterised strongman controlling it and these has a lot of influence over those living there

You are a walking symbol pointing to where you were born: - Shade – eyes - colour of skin - texture of hair - style of clothing - eating habit - speech

If your life is affected by sterility, barrenness, constant lack of success and failure to gain any sort of ascendancy no matter how hard you try then a curse may be in operation. If you think this may be the case then do some research on your life and family history and take the matter before the Lord.

Therefore, a curse is a terrible thing. It has a backing force and what you can call an enforcing spirit.

You need to know how to destroy it. And immediately you begin to do that, your trouble will be in trouble.

Curses, spell or sanction is of the devil and are not in line with God's plans for you. It could be that somebody, either dead or living is responsible for it. There are different kinds of curses, spells or sanctions. Known curses or unknown curses, inherited curses or direct curses, location curses, move into or trade into (Sex). Association curse or hereditary. (City, town and Nation curse) but what I know is that the curse upon you can turn to blessing. Ps. 109:28.

CHAPTER TWO: A CURSE WITH A CAUSE

If a curse is working in our life, it will always have a cause. Proverbs 26:2 says

'Like a sparrow in its flitting and a swallow in its flying so a curse without a cause CANNOT alight.'

By reading Deuteronomy 28 and Leviticus 26, one can find many curses (and blessings) listed. It would do well for each one of us to examine which curses (and blessings) are applicable in our own lives.

Unfortunately, there are those who do not believe a Christian can be under a curse. All they need to do is read I Corinthians 11:27-31 where it says a believer who takes the Lord's Supper with unconfessed and unrepented sin in his life, can be weak, sick, and even die.

'Wherefore whosoever shall eat this bread, and drink this cup of the Lord, unworthily, shall be guilty of the body and blood of the Lord. But let a man examine himself, and so let him eat of that bread, and drink of that cup. For he that eateth and drinketh unworthily, eateth and drinketh damnation to himself, not discerning the Lord's body. For this cause many are weak and sickly among you, and many sleep (deceased/die). '

"My people are destroyed for lack of knowledge: because thou hast rejected knowledge." (Hosea 4:6)

There are many who mistakenly believe because these verses are found in the Old Testament, they are not relevant today. However, 2 Timothy 3:15-18 (as well as many other verses) dispels this lie. It says:

"All Scripture is inspired by God and profitable for teaching, for reproof, for correction, for training in righteousness; so that the man of God may be adequate, equipped for every good work."

Sadly, whether we choose to believe it or not, curses do exist in a believer's life. Curses come about through iniquity and iniquity from sin. In other words, when an individual transgresses God's law, then it creates an iniquity in him and that iniquity is, therefore, passed to his children. It causes weakness or bent toward that certain behavior or you may continuously yield toward that temptation which is passed from generation to generation. That certain iniquity will continue to affect that particular bloodline until someone in the bloodline takes accountability for it, confesses it as sin and appropriates the blood of Jesus over it.

Exodus 20:5 "Thou shalt not bow down thyself to them [idols], nor serve them: for I the LORD thy God am a jealous God, visiting the iniquity of the fathers upon the children unto the third and fourth generation of them that hate me."

I Corinthians 3:9 says: "For we are God's fellow workers; you are God's field, God's building".

 Isaiah 5:7 says: "The vineyard of the LORD of hosts is the house of Israel and the men of Judah His delightful plant".

Hosea 10:12 instructs us to, "Sow with a view to righteousness, reap in accordance with kindness; break up your fallow ground, for it is time to seek the LORD until He comes to rain righteousness on you."

Curses and blessings are often like seeds planted in a garden. They may be evil or good. They are planted deep within the soil of your soul (your mind, will and emotions). Seeds planted can come from your childhood or from your fore-fathers, planted within you before you are born, either producing good or bad fruits.

Certainly, each one of us can be sure there is a curse working in his or her life when we find ourselves being overcome, defeated, bitter, angry, hurt, fearful, terrorized, sick, mentally ill, addicted, depressed, confused, discouraged, etc., and in the midst of this attack, there appears to be no healing or permanent relief for our problem. If this is the case, we need to seek God for the unresolved hidden cause(s) of the curse. The cause may not only be our own sin, but also the generational iniquity of our forefathers. We must confess our own personal sin (what we are reaping) and that of our fore-fathers.

"We acknowledge, O LORD, our wickedness, and the iniquity of our fathers: for we have sinned against thee." Jeremiah 14:20

Praise God that when the sin behind the curse is dealt with (confessed and cut at the root), victory, as well as healing, will come. I often tell others that this is one major reason why going to the world for help (to hang in there) does not remove the curse or the demon(s) behind the curse. It is likened to removing the spider web, but allowing the spider to remain! It simply puts a big temporary worldly bandage on a spiritual problem!

If a curse is working in your life, there is a cause. If you are not careful to observe all the words of this law, which are written in this book, to fear this honoured and awesome name, the LORD your God, then the LORD will bring extraordinary plagues on you and your descendants, even severe and lasting plagues, and miserable and chronic sicknesses (Deut. 28:58-60). This scripture clearly indicates that sicknesses stem from curses. Simply put, demons carry out the curses and holy angels carry out the blessings.

2 Timothy 3:12 says:

"Yea, and all that will live godly in Christ Jesus shall suffer persecution."

However, the Bible also promises that even in the midst of persecution, we can be victorious! Praise God! It does not matter, whatever happens to us, regardless of what we suffer or go through, all of it is for the purpose of conforming us into the image of Christ! We CAN have overcoming victory. We can turn the wrong responses and attitudes around and manifest the character and nature of Jesus. (Romans 8:33-39)

The difference between a fiery dart from the enemy and a curse is this: If it is just a fiery dart, taking up the shield of faith (being in God's refuge through dying to the flesh) dispels the attack of the enemy and victory is won. "For You (God) have been a defense for the helpless, A defense for the needy in his distress, A refuge from the storm, a shade from the heat; for the breath of the ruthless is like a rain storm against a wall." (Isaiah 25:4)

"They that trust in the LORD shall be as mount Zion, which cannot be removed, but abideth forever. As the mountains are round about Jerusalem, so the LORD is round about his people from henceforth even forever. For the rod (dart) of the wicked shall not rest (stay, remain, abide) upon the lot of the righteous; lest the righteous put forth their hands unto iniquity. Do good, O LORD, unto those that be good, and to them that are upright in their hearts. As for such as turn aside unto their crooked ways, the LORD shall lead them forth with the workers of iniquity: but peace shall be upon Israel (the Church)." (Psalm 125:1-5)

"Thou wilt keep him in perfect peace, whose mind is stayed on thee: because he trusteth in thee." (Isaiah 26:3)

 "And the rain descended, and the floods came, and the winds blew, and beat upon that house; and it fell not: for it was founded upon a rock..". (Matthew 7:25)

"When a man's ways please the Lord, it makes even his enemies to be at peace with him." (Proverbs 16:7)

"A rebellious man seeks only evil so a cruel messenger will be sent against him." (Proverbs 17:11)

"He who dwells in the secret place of the Most High God shall abide under the shadow and protection of the Almighty... Because we make the Lord our refuge, even the Most High our habitation, no evil will befall us and no plague will come neigh our dwelling." (Psalms 91:1,11)

"Where then does wisdom come from? And where is the place of understanding? Thus it is hidden from the eyes of all living and concealed from the birds of the sky" (Job 28:20-21)

"But thou, O LORD, be merciful unto me, and raise me up, that I may requite them. By this I know that thou favourest me, because mine enemy doth not triumph over me." (Psalms 41:10-11)

"Arise, O' LORD, disappoint him, cast him down: deliver my soul from the wicked which is

THY SWORD." (Psalm 17:13)

A good way to describe our dilemma could be likened to a house with windows wide open, giving entrance to the enemy. As each window is closed through repentance, the enemy's entryway is being closed off. No longer does he have a legal right, except in the areas where the windows are left open. The Lord does not show us all the open windows (hidden places) at once; only those He has appointed next on His sanctifying list.

God drives the enemy out little by little (window by window). He uses the problems in our lives, (if we are wise enough to ask Him) not only for the purpose of conforming us into His image, but also to reveal unresolved issues. As those issues crop up, He expects us to deal with them heads on. Remember, Jesus already won the victory for us at Calvary and paid the price for our sanctification; but in order for us to work it out, (totally by His grace) it takes a lifetime.

"Wherefore, my beloved, as ye have always obeyed, not as in my presence only, but now much more in my absence, work out your own salvation (deliverance from the molestation of the enemy) with fear and trembling." (Philippians 2:12)

Exodus 23:27-30 confirms that sanctification is a process. It says:

"I will send my fear before thee, and will destroy all the people to whom thou shalt come, and I will make all thine enemies turn their backs unto thee. And I will send hornets before thee which shall drive out the Hivite, the Canaanite, and the Hittite, from before thee (enemies). I will not drive them out from before thee in one year; lest the land become desolate, and the beast of the field multiply against thee. By little and little I will drive them out from before thee, until thou be increased, and inherit the land."

Be encouraged! If you are not into willful sin and things appear not be going as expected, be mindful that God is not mad at you. It simply means that there are issues that He wants you to see about yourself or from the generations before you. He loves you so much. It is necessary He cleans you up for your highest good and for His greatest glory! His eyes are too pure to look upon and tolerate our sin. Those whom the Lord loves, he disciplines, and he scourges every son whom he receives (Hebrews 12:6)

STRONGHOLDS OF CURSE (Why some curse is difficult to break)

Many Christian cannot command in the place of prayer because of:

Hidden sin.

Unsanctified mouth and tongue (Jer. 1:9-10, Song of Solomon6:6-7)

Nonpayment of tithe, a vow and pledges (Job22:27-28)

Not having good account with God (1Kings 17:1-2)?

Stand farmed in God presents; Jonah fled from God's presence (Jonah 1:3), and God called

Abraham after 25 years that he been following God and he said to him, walk before me and thou be perfect. (Gen. 17:1-27).Can you say you stand before God?

Ignorance.

Fear.

Because their spiritual battery is uncharged try to recharge your battery in prayer, fasting, bible study, worship and fellowship with God.

You need higher power or cooperate anointing; These people chose Elisha because his anointing was comparable to that of Joshua. So, if a powerful native doctor puts a curse upon somebody, he or she would need a person with a higher anointing to break it.

CHAPTER THREE: HOW TO PREVENT CURSES FROM HAVING EFFECT ON YOUR LIFE

Overcoming the forces of limitation does not depend on God alone. The responsibilities are laid on you and I. It is a matter of choice!

"For whatever is born of God overcomes the world. And this is the victory that has overcome the world; our faith". {1st John 5: 4-5}

Isaiah 22:25.

In that day, saith the Lord of hosts, shall the nail that is fastened in the sure place be removed, and be cut down, and fall; and the burden that was upon it shall be cut off: for the Lord hath spoken it

The scriptures reveal a number of ways in which we can break curses and or be protected from them, but be aware that

A curse can be canceled. (Galatians 3:13-14)

A curse can be diverted (psalms 109:28)

A curse can be suspended

A curse can be transferred. (Isaiah 39:7-8)

Curse is contagious (2 kings 5:27)

A curse can be inherited (1 kings 16:34)

A curse can be prevented

A curse can be transferred to another Isaiah 39:5-8.

A curse can be reversed (2 kings 2:19-22)

One can be immunized against a curse. (Psalms 109:28, Galatians 6:17)

To stop curses from having an effect on us, we must do the following:

HOW TO STOP THOSE CURSES

Surrender your life to Jesus Christ.

Repent from your sins.

Repent from your Forefather's sins.

Break the soul tie with any curse.

You need to command the demons of that curse to leave you.

Break yourself out of the curse.

There are many Bible verses on curses in the scriptures and the above list just touches on some of the main causes and their remedies. Basically, a curse can only alight on an area that God has already judged as being worthy of a curse, such as incest, idolatry or murder. Most curses generally last only 3-4 generations; though, some have lasted since creation. Repentance from sin, breaking ties with the occult and taking refuge in Christ who has become a curse for us are the main strategies we can use to break curses.

Live a righteous life free from sin and acts of injustice. Abide in the righteousness of Christ where no curse can penetrate (Malachi 4:6; Proverbs 26:2; Romans 8).

Put on the full armour of God as contained in Ephesians 6:10-21 which is actually armour against spiritual attack. Ephesus was noted for its magic practices (Acts 19) and its curses and witchcraft. The primary purpose behind Paul writing to the Ephesians was that so they could have some understanding of their power, authority, and degree of protection in their pagan and occult city. The armour of God is like the Kevlar of the spirit world protecting the Christian against curses, magic, and occult practices.

Part of this is putting on the whole armour of God which is designed to protect us from curses leveled against us in the course of spiritual warfare (Ephesians 6:10-18). When the curse is lifted, then the human spirit that has been affected by the curse and bowed down with pain, confusion, and futility will be quickly healed. The person will recover and emotional normality would soon follow.

Reversing their evil curses: God is able to turn a curse into a blessing. He did this when Balak tried to get Baalam to curse Israel (Nehemiah 13:2; Deuteronomy 23:5; Numbers 22&23). A brief prayer by Jabez that has received a lot of popularity lately is a case of a person appealing to God to have a curse turned into blessing and success. David is particularly bold when he said in Psalm 109 where he seemed to have been the victim of a curse (see verses 17 & 18) (Psalms 109:28 NKJV) Let them curse, but you bless; When they arise, let them be ashamed, But let your servant rejoice. David did not fear the curse but instead asked God to bless him and outdo the curse, and then to turn the curse back on those who uttered it. God can out bless the most fearsome and disabling curses. It gives us hope that our prayers to God based on the name of Jesus cannot only break curses but have them turned into blessings instead.

Understand and plead the fact that Christ has taken all the curses due to us when He became a curse on the cross (Galatians 3:10-14). That in Christ, ground for curses to succeed against us is removed because, on the cross, Jesus became a curse for us and took all the cursing that may have been due to us owing to our violation of God's laws.

Break associations with the sins of parents and ancestors, particularly those involving the occult or idolatry. Exodus 34:6,7 says such sins bring a curse "to the third and fourth generations". We have to break ties with such sins by not participating in occult ceremonies that may be traditional and even confessing such involvement of your parents and ancestors and forsaking them in a prayer of renunciation to God. The essential thing is to make a clear break with the familial sin in your own heart, mind, and spirit.

Get rid of objects that bring a curse, particularly objects associated with pagan worship, idolatry or the occult. For instance, if we have our grandmother's pack of tarot cards, we need to get rid of them (Deuteronomy 7:25, 26) The Ephesian converts were moved by the Holy Spirit to burn their magic scrolls and occultic objects (Acts 19:18-20).

Do not engage in secret sins that you think you can get away with unobserved. In Deuteronomy 27: 15-26, certain sins are singled out as capable of bringing curses, notably the making of idols, incest, bestiality, treating parents with contempt, injustice against migrants, widows, the disabled or the poor, hiring a contract killer, and moving your neighbours landmark or boundary stones. Most of these are crimes that would never be tried in court because of the secret nature of the crimes, lack of two or three eyewitnesses willing to testify or the difficulty of proving the case such as 'my word against yours' case of the boundary stone. The curse was God's way of making sure that such secret crimes did not go unpunished. People knew that if they did these things, God would repay. Even in the New Testament, God is referred to as the one who punishes those who defile the marriage bed. (1 Thessalonians 4:4-6; Hebrews 13:4). If you have done any of the things in the above list, then repentance, restoration and an earnest appeal to God for mercy would be a good starting point in breaking the curse over your life.

Put God's interests ahead of your own. In the book of Haggai, God put a curse on the nation (Haggai 1:5-11; 2:16-17) for being self-centered and neglectful of their duty to God. The curse was removed when the people obeyed the prophets and laid the foundation of the Lord's temple (Haggai 2:18-19) and a blessing was given instead.

HOW TO PREVENT CURSES FROM HAVING EFFECT ON YOUR LIFE

The scriptures reveal a number of ways in which we can break curses and or be protected from them.

There are many Bible verses on curses in the scriptures and the above list just touches on some of the main causes and their remedies. Basically, a curse can only alight on an area that God has already judged as being worthy of a curse, such as incest, idolatry or murder. Most curses generally last only 3-4 generations; though, some have lasted since creation. Repentance from sin, breaking ties with the occult and taking refuge in Christ who has become a curse for us are the main strategies we can use to break curses.

Live a righteous life free from major sin and acts of injustice. Abide in the righteousness of Christ where no curse can penetrate (Malachi 4:6; Proverbs 26:2; Romans 8).

Put on the full armour of God as contained in Ephesians 6 :10-21 which is actually armour against spiritual attack. Ephesus was noted for its magic practices (Acts 19) and its curses and witchcraft. The primary purpose behind Paul writing to the Ephesians was that so they could have some understanding of their power, authority and degree of protection in their pagan and occult city. The armour of God is like the Kevlar of the spirit world protecting the Christian against curses, magic and occult practices.

Part of this is putting on the whole armour of God which is designed to protect us from curses levelled against us in the course of spiritual warfare (Ephesians 6:10-18). When the curse is lifted, then the human spirit that has been affected by the curse and bowed down with pain, confusion and futility will be quickly healed. The person will recover and emotional normality would soon follow.

Revising their evil curses: God is able to turn a curse into a blessing. He did this when Balak tried to get Baalam to curse Israel (Nehemiah 13:2; Deuteronomy 23:5; Numbers 22&23). A brief prayer by Jabez that has received a lot of popularity lately is a case of a person appealing to God to have a curse turned into blessing and success. David is particularly bold when he said in Psalm 109 where he seemed to have been the victim of a curse (see verses 17 & 18) (Psalms 109:28 NKJV) Let them curse, but you bless; When they arise, let them be ashamed, But let your servant rejoice. David did not fear the curse, but instead asked God to bless him and outdo the curse, and then to turn the curse back on those who uttered it. God can outbless the most fearsome and disabling curses. It gives us hope that our prayers to God based on the name of Jesus cannot only break curses, but have them turned into blessings instead.

Understand and plead the fact that Christ has taken all the curses due to us when He became a curse on the cross (Galatians 3:10-14). That in Christ, ground for curses to succeed against us is removed because on the cross, Jesus became a curse for us and took all the cursing that may have been due to us owing to our violation of God's laws.

Break associations with the sins of parents and ancestors, particularly those involving the occult or idolatry. Exodus 34:6,7 says such sins bring a curse "to the third and fourth generations". We have to break ties with such sins by not participating in occult ceremonies that may be traditional and even confessing such involvement of your parents and ancestors and forsaking them in a prayer of renunciation to God. The essential thing is to make a clear break with the familial sin in your own heart, mind and spirit.

Get rid of objects that bring a curse, particularly objects associated with pagan worship, idolatry or the occult. For instance, if we have our grandmother's pack of tarot cards, we need to get rid of them (Deuteronomy 7:25, 26) The Ephesian converts were moved by the Holy Spirit to burn their magic scrolls and occultic objects (Acts 19:18-20).

Do not engage in secret or dishonest sins that you think you can get away with unobserved. In Deuteronomy 27: 15-26, certain sins are singled out as capable of bringing curses, notably the making of idols, incest, bestiality, treating parents with contempt, injustice against migrants, widows, the disabled or the poor, hiring a contract killer, and moving your neighbours landmark or boundary stones. Most of these are crimes that would never be tried in court because of the secret nature of the crimes, lack of two or three eye witnesses willing to testify or the difficulty of proving the case such as 'my word against yours' case of the boundary stone.

The curse was God's way of making sure that such secret crimes did not go unpunished. People knew that if they did these things, God would repay. Even in the New Testament, God is referred to as the one who punishes those who defile the marriage bed. (1 Thessalonians 4:4-6; Hebrews 13:4). If you have done any of the things in the above list, then repentance, restoration and an earnest appeal to God for mercy would be a good starting point in breaking the curse over your life.

Put God's interests ahead of your own. In the book of Haggai, God put a curse on the nation (Haggai 1:5-11; 2:16-17) for being self-centered and neglectful of their duty to God. The curse was removed when the people obeyed the prophets and laid the foundation on the Lord's temple (Haggai 2:18-19) and a blessing was given instead.

There are certain curses that work against life (Deut. 27:14-26).

So, what you need to do basically, is to restitute your ways (Judges 17:1-13; Gen. 35:1-4).

You can also use the word of God to rewrite your record by revoking the evil spell.

You should learn to claim the blessings of God and look for a man of God for prayers of faith.

Live holy and restitute your ways

One of the ways to prevent curses is by destroying curses. Your mouth contains a double barrel power.

Another way to prevent curses is that the words you speak can destroy or promote you. When a man who has a backing force speaks some words, those words can cause trouble. The words you now speak, backed up by the force, can limit a life or explode a destiny.

Another way to prevent curses is to get rid of sin from your life. In anything you are doing, you must remember that God is the Lord of harvest. You cannot live in sin and expect prosperity; you cannot cheat people and prosper. An adulterous man who does not repent would one day impregnate a woman outside marriage and that child of adultery would move into the family and dismantle the structures he has put up. Anybody who is living in sin is sowing evil and as he sows evil, he would reap evil. So, sin is terrible.

Investigate your family history. Some people have what can be called family sins. For example, Abraham told Abimelech that Sarah, his wife, was his sister. Forty years later, Isaac told the same Abimelech that his wife was his sister. Sixty years later, Jacob and his mother deceived their father. Eighty years later, Jacob's children deceived him that Joseph was dead. Hundred years later, Judah slept with his daughter in-law who deceived him. So, you need to confess every personal and ancestral sins and get rid of them fast.

THE CURSELESS PERSONALITIES

You are curseless if you first terminate the inherited and prevent any other one.

Psalm 109:28: "Let them curse, but bless thou: when they arise, let them be ashamed; but let thy servant rejoice."

Numbers 23:23: Surely, there is no enchantment against Jacob, neither is there any divination against Israel: according to this time it shall be said of Jacob and of Israel, What hath God wrought!"

1 Sam. 17:43 "And the Philistine said unto David, Am I a dog, that thou comest to me with staves? And the Philistine cursed David by his gods".

1 Samuel 17:44-47

44. And the Philistine said to David, Come to me, and I will give thy flesh unto the fowls of the air, and to the beasts of the field.

45. Then said David to the Philistine, Thou comest to me with a sword, and with a spear, and with a shield: but I come to thee in the name of the LORD of hosts, the God of the armies of Israel, whom thou hast defied.

46. This day will the LORD deliver thee into mine hand; and I will smite thee, and take thine head from thee; and I will give the carcasses of the host of the Philistines this day unto the fowls of the air, and to the wild beasts of the earth; that all the earth may know that there is a God in Israel.

47. And all this assembly shall know that the LORD saveth not with sword and spear: for the battle is the LORD's, and he will give you into our hands.

Why did you accept breakdown in life, when you can live in perpetual victory?

Jesus answered them, "Is it not written in your law, I said, Ye are gods? If he called them gods, unto whom the word of God came, and the scripture cannot be broken." (John 10:34-35)

The Bible says we are gods, even Jesus confirmed it, If you are a god, you resemble your father (Lion beget Lion, goat beget goat, dog beget dog)

You can create like your father because you have divine nature of God in your life. (John14:12; Acts 10:38)

You have a say over your situation (2king 2:19-21).

As a man thinketh (Proverbs 23:7).

Death and life are in the power of the tongue (Proverbs 18:21).

And Jacob took his rods of green poplar, and of the hazel and chew nut tree; and pilled white strakes in them, and made the white appear which was in the rods.

And he set the rods which he had pilled before the flocks in the gutters in the watering troughs when the flocks came to drink, that they should conceive when they came to drink. And the flocks conceived before the rods, and brought forth cattle rings raked, speckled, and spotted. And Jacob did separate the lambs, and set the faces of the flocks toward the rings raked, and all the brown in the flock of Laban; and he put his own flocks by themselves, and put them not unto

Laban's cattle. And it came to pass, whatsoever the stronger cattle did conceive, that Jacob laid the rods before the eyes of the cattle in the gutters that they might conceive among the rods. But when the cattle were feeble, he put them not in: so the feebler were Laban's, and the stronger Jacob's. And the man increased exceedingly, and had much cattle, and maidservants, and menservants, and camels, and asses (Who taught Jacob to use the rod? (Genesis 30:37-43?)

You have power over poverty, sickness, evil forces, your enemy, sorrow and sin (Romans 6:12-14). But if you don't use it, it becomes useless (he who can read, but reads not is not better than the stack illiterate).

WHAT IS THE WAY OUT OF STUBBORN CURSES?

Surrender your life to Jesus. You need His power to break evil curses. James 4:7.

Confess your sins and those of your ancestors.

Forgive yourself and others.

Renounce all attachment and involvement with curses.

Break all links and contacts with the enemy.
For example break evil soul ties and blood covenants properly and thoroughly.

Return all accursed properties or they will act as a ladder that keeps allowing the enemy back in. Satan will keep coming back so long as his property is in there.

Release yourself from all curses standing on your redemption through the blood of Jesus.Galatians 3:13-14, Colossians 2:14-15.

Replace curses with blessings.

Be obedient to God and His word.

Live a holy and righteous life to prevent reinforcement, regrouping, and counter attack.

Barricade you're your life with the blood of Jesus and the fire of God so that they not find their way back into your life and destiny.

CHAPTER FOUR: LET US PRAY

CONFESS OUT, LOUD SCRIPTURES PROMISING DELIVERANCE

Warfare Scriptures:

(Proverbs 26:2).As the bird by wandering, as the swallow by flying, so the curse causeless shall not come.

Deut. 33:25-27 says, "Thy shoes shall be iron and brass; and as thy days, so shall thy strength be. [26] There is none like unto the God of Jeshurun, who rideth upon the heaven in thy help, and in his excellency on the sky. [27] The eternal God is thy refuge, and underneath are the everlasting arms: and he shall thrust out the enemy from before thee; and shall say, Destroy them."

Isaiah 28:18: "And your covenant with death shall be disannulled, and your agreement with hell shall not stand; when the overflowing scourge shall pass through, then ye shall be trodden down by it."

Isaiah 49:24-26: "Shall the prey be taken from the mighty, or the lawful captive delivered? 25 But thus saith the LORD, Even the captives of the mighty shall be taken away, and the prey of the terrible shall be delivered: for I will contend with him that contendeth with thee, and I will save thy children. 26 And I will feed them that oppress thee with their own flesh; and they shall be drunken with their own blood, as with sweet wine: and all flesh shall know that I the LORD am thy Saviour and thy Redeemer, the mighty One of Jacob."

Isaiah 54:14-17 "…thou shall be far from oppression: for thou shall not fear: and from terror; for it shall not come near thee" says, "Behold, they shall surely gather together, but not by me: whosoever shall gather together against thee shall fall for thy sake. No weapon that is formed against thee shall prosper; and every tongue that shall rise against thee in judgment thou shalt condemn. This is the heritage of the servants of the Lord, and their righteousness is of me, saith the Lord."

Isaiah 54:4 "Fear not; for thou shalt not be ashamed: neither be thou confounded; for thou shalt not be put to shame: for thou shalt forget the shame of thy youth, and shalt not remember the reproach of thy widowhood anymore."

Isaiah 54:5 "For thy Maker is thine husband; the LORD of hosts is his name; and thy Redeemer the Holy One of Israel; The God of the whole earth shall he be called." [Therefore if Jesus is your husband, then legally and according to Him, you cannot have any other marine husband or wife]

Isaiah 59:19 says, "So shall they fear the name of the Lord from the west, and his glory from the rising of the sun. When the enemy shall come in like a flood, the Spirit of the Lord shall lift up a standard against him."

Isaiah 55:11 "So shall my word be that goeth forth out of my mouth: it shall not return unto me void, but it shall accomplish that which I please, and it shall prosper in the thing whereto I sent it."

Jeremiah 30:16-17 says, "Therefore all they that devour thee shall be devoured; and all thine adversaries, every one of them, shall go into captivity; and they that spoil thee shall be a spoil, and all that prey upon thee will I give for a prey. [17] For I will restore health unto thee, and I will heal thee of thy wounds, saith the Lord; because they called thee an Outcast, saying, This is Zion, whom no man seeketh after."

Matt. 28:8 And Jesus came and spake unto them, saying, All power is given unto me in heaven and in earth.

Proverbs 26:2 - As the bird by wandering, as the swallow by flying, so the curse causeless shall not come.

Psalm 27:2 says, "When the wicked, even mine enemies and my foes, came upon me to eat up my flesh, they stumbled and fell."

Psalm 35:8 says, "Let destruction come upon him at unawares; and let his net that he hath hid catch himself: into that very destruction let him fall."

Psalm 91:3: "Surely he shall deliver thee from the snare of the fowler, and from the noisome pestilence."

Psalm 124: 7 Our soul is escaped as a bird out of the snare of the fowlers: the snare is broken, and we are escaped.

Psalm 129: 4 The Lord is righteous: he hath cut asunder the cords of the wicked. 5 Let them all be confounded and turned back that hate Zion.

Psalm 35:4 Let them be confounded and put to shame that seek after my soul: let them be turned back and brought to confusion that devise my hurt. 5 Let them be as chaff before the wind: and let the angel of the Lord chase them. 6 Let their way be dark and slippery: and let the angel of the Lord persecute them.

Psalm 56:9 When I cry unto thee, then shall mine enemies turn back: this I know; for God is for me.

Psalm 91: 13 Thou shalt tread upon the lion and adder: the young lion and the dragon shalt thou trample under feet.

Psalm 68:1-2 says, "Let God arise, let his enemies be scattered: let them also that hate him flee before him. [2] As smoke is driven away, so drive them away: as wax melteth before the fire, so let the wicked perish at the presence of God."

Isaiah 62:2-3: And the Gentiles shall see thy righteousness, and all the kings thy glory: and thou shalt be called by a new name, which the month of the Lord shall name. Thou shalt also be a crown of glory in the hand of the Lord, and a royal diadem in the hand of thy God.

Obadiah 1:3-4 says, "The pride of thine heart hath deceived thee, thou that dwellest in the clefts of the rock, whose habitation is high; that saith in his heart, Who shall bring me down to the ground? [4] Though thou exalt thyself as the eagle, and though thou set thy nest among the stars, thence will I bring thee down, saith the Lord."

Isaiah 50:7-9 says, "For the Lord God will help me; therefore shall I not be confounded: therefore have I set my face like a flint, and I know that I shall not be ashamed. [8] He is near that justifieth me; who will contend with me? let us stand together: who is mine adversary? let him come near to me. [9] Behold, the Lord God will help me; who is he that shall condemn me? lo, they all shall wax old as a garment; the moth shall eat them up."

Isaiah 8:8-10 says, "And he shall pass through Judah; he shall overflow and go over, he shall reach even to the neck; and the stretching out of his wings shall fill the breadth of thy land, O Immanuel. [9] Associate yourselves, O ye people, and ye shall be broken in pieces; and give ear, all ye of far countries: gird yourselves, and ye shall be broken in pieces; gird yourselves, and ye shall be broken in pieces. [10] Take counsel together, and it shall come to nought; speak the word, and it shall not stand: for God is with us."

Joshua 1:5 says, "There shall not any man be able to stand before thee all the days of thy life: as I was with Moses, so I will be with thee: I will not fail thee, nor forsake thee."

Ephesians 1:7: "In whom we have redemption through his blood, the forgiveness of sins, according to the riches of his grace."

Jeremiah 1:10,19 says, "See, I have this day set thee over the nations and over the kingdoms, to root out, and to pull down, and to destroy, and to throw down, to build, and to plant. And they shall fight against thee; but they shall not prevail against thee; for I am with thee, saith the Lord, to deliver thee."

Col 2: 14 blotting out the handwriting of ordinances that was against us, which was contrary to us, and took it out of the way, nailing it to his cross; 15 and having spoiled principalities and powers, he made a show of them openly, triumphing over them in it.

Colossians 2:14,15: "Blotting out the handwriting of ordinances that was against us, which was contrary to us, and took it out of the way, nailing it to his cross;   15 And having spoiled principalities and powers, he made a show of them openly, triumphing over them in it."

Col. 2:15: and having spoiled principalities and powers, he made shew of then openly, triumphing over them in it.

Hebrew. 2:15:   and deliver them who through fear of death were all their life-time subject to bondage.

Matthew 3:10 says, "And now also the axe is laid unto the root of the trees: therefore every tree which bringeth not forth good fruit is hewn down, and cast into the fire."

Gal 3:13-14: Christ hath redeemed us from the curse of the law, being made a curse for us: for it is written, Cursed is every one that hangeth on a tree: That the blessing of Abraham might come on the Gentiles through Jesus Christ; that we might receive the promise of the Spirit through faith.

Galatians 3:13-14: "Christ hath redeemed us from the curse of the law, being made a curse for us: for it is written, Cursed is every one that hangeth on a tree: 14 That the blessing of Abraham might come on the Gentiles through Jesus Christ; that we might receive the promise of the Spirit through faith."

Zech. 4:7 says, "Who art thou, O great mountain? before Zerubbabel thou shalt become a plain: and he shall bring forth the headstone thereof with shoutings, crying, Grace, grace unto it."

2 Tim. 4:18 says, "And the Lord shall deliver me from every evil work, and will preserve me unto his heavenly kingdom: to whom be glory for ever and ever. Amen."

2 Tim. 4:18: "And the Lord shall deliver me from every evil work, and will preserve me unto His heavenly kingdom: to whom be glory for ever and ever. Amen."

Ephesians 4:27 - Neither give place to the devil.

Joshua 5:9 "This day have I rolled away the reproach of Egypt from off you." [Remind God of His word and claim it for yourself]

Job 5:12 says, "He disappointeth the devices of the crafty, so that their hands cannot perform their enterprise."

2 Corinthians 5:17 - Therefore if any man [be] in Christ, [he is] a new creature: old things are passed away; behold, all things are become new.

Ephesians 6:12 - For we wrestle not against flesh and blood, but against principalities, against powers, against the rulers of the darkness of this world, against spiritual wickedness in high [places].

Joshua 6:26, "And Joshua adjured them at that time, saying, Cursed be the man before the Lord, that riseth up and buildeth this city Jericho: he shall lay the foundation thereof in his firstborn, and in his youngest son shall he set up the gates of it"

Psalm 7:15-16 says, "He made a pit, and digged it, and is fallen into the ditch which he made. [16] His mischief shall return upon his own head, and his violent dealing shall come down upon his own pate."

Capernaum   (Mark 8:22) – And he cometh to Bethsaida; and they bring a blind man unto him, and besought him to touch him. And he took the blind man by the hand, and led him out of the town; and when he had spit on his eyes, and put his hands upon him, he asked him if he saw ought. And he looked up, and said, I see men as trees, walking. After that he put his hands again upon his eyes, and made him look up: and he was restored, and saw every man clearly. And he sent him away to his house, saying, Neither go into the town, nor tell it to any in the town.

Luke 10: 18 And he said unto them, I beheld Satan as lightning fall from heaven. 19 Behold, I give unto you power to tread on serpents and scorpions, and over all the power of the enemy: and nothing shall by any means hurt you.

Luke 10:19: "Behold, I give unto you power to tread on serpents and scorpions, and over all the power of the enemy: and nothing shall by any means hurt you."

Psm 11: 6 Upon the wicked he shall rain snares, fire and brimstone, and an horrible tempest: this shall be the portion of their cup. 7 For the righteous Lord loveth righteousness; his countenance doth behold the upright.

Matthew 11:20-24, "Then began he to upbraid the cities wherein most of his mighty works were done, because they repented not: Woe unto thee, Chorazin! woe unto thee, Bethsaida! for if the mighty works, which were done in you, had been done in Tyre and Sidon, they would have repented long ago in sackcloth and ashes. But I say unto you, It shall be more tolerable for Tyre and Sidon at the day of judgment, than for you. And thou, Capernaum, which art exalted unto heaven, shalt be brought down to hell: for if the mighty works, which have been done in thee, had been done in Sodom, it would have remained until this day. But I say unto you, That it shall be more tolerable for the land of Sodom in the day of judgment, than for thee."

Revelation 12:11: "And they overcame him by the blood of the Lamb, and by the word of their testimony; and they loved not their lives unto the death."

Rev. 13:10 says, "He that leadeth into captivity shall go into captivity: he that killeth with the sword must be killed with the sword. Here is the patience and the faith of the saints."

Matthew 16:19 - And I will give unto thee the keys of the kingdom of heaven: and whatsoever thou shalt bind on earth shall be bound in heaven: and whatsoever thou shalt loose on earth shall be loosed in heaven.

Rm 16: 20 And the God of peace shall bruise Satan under your feet shortly. The grace of our Lord Jesus Christ be with you.

Romans 16:20: "And the God of peace shall bruise Satan under your feet shortly. The grace of our Lord Jesus Christ be with you. Amen."

Jeremiah 17:18 says, "Let them be confounded that persecute me, but let not me be confounded: let them be dismayed, but let not me be dismayed: bring upon them the day of evil, and destroy them with double destruction."

Psm18:17 He delivered me from my strong enemy, and from them which hated me: for they were too strong for me.

Ezekiel 18:19-20 - Yet say ye, Why? Doth not the son bear the iniquity of the father? When the son hath done that which is lawful and right, [and] hath kept all my statutes, and hath done them, he shall surely live.

Psm 18: 37 I have pursued mine enemies, and overtaken them: neither did I turn again till they were consumed. 38 I have wounded them that they were not able to rise: they are fallen under my feet. 39 For thou hast girded me with strength unto the battle: thou hast subdued under me those that rose up against me. 40 Thou hast also given me the necks of mine enemies; that I might destroy them that hate me.

Psalm 18:44-45 says, "As soon as they hear of me, they shall obey me: the strangers shall submit themselves unto me. [45] The strangers shall fade away, and be afraid out of their close places."

Numbers 23:23 says, "Surely there is no enchantment against Jacob, neither is there any divination against Israel: according to this time it shall be said of Jacob and of Israel, What hath God wrought!"

Isaiah 41:10-12 says, "Fear thou not; for I am with thee: be not dismayed; for I am thy God: I will strengthen thee; yea, I will help thee; yea, I will uphold thee with the right hand of my righteousness. [11] Behold, all they that were incensed against thee shall be ashamed and confounded: they shall be as nothing; and they that strive with thee shall perish. [12] Thou shalt seek them, and shalt not find them, even them that contended with thee: they that war against thee shall be as nothing, and as a thing of nought."

PRAYER POINTS

 The devil smiles when we plan, he laughs when we get too busy. but he trembles when we pray

All curses of evil powers of the night, be broken in the name of Jesus.

All curses of the evil powers of the night, be broken, in the name of Jesus.

All demonic spirits and powers involved (name them if they've been discerned), I bind you and command you to cease your activity in my life and to leave my life, my body, my soul, my mind, my family, my house, my job, etc.

All demonic spirits attached to all evil covenants and curses operating against my
life, be roasted by fire of God, in the name of Jesus.

All demonic spirits attached to all these covenants and curses, be roasted with the fire of God, in the name of Jesus

All the doors of blessings and break-through shat against me due to my past
involvement in these evil associations, I command you to open in the name of
Jesus.

Any ancestral blood shed of animals, or human beings affecting me, loose your hold by the blood of Jesus.

Any connecting link between me and any power of darkness, break by fire in the name of Jesus.

Any Covenant with the waters against my life break in Jesus Name.

Any curse hanging on my family tree, break in the name of Jesus.

Any curse placed on my ancestors by anybody cheated or maltreated at the point of death, break and release me now in the name of Jesus

Any curse placed on my ancestral line by anybody cheated, maltreated or at the point of death, break now, in Jesus' name.

Any curse that has hijack my family history, break in Jesus Name.

Any curse under which my family labour, be broken by the power in the blood of Jesus.

Any curse, place on my ancestors by anybody cheated, maltreated at the point of death, break and release me now in the name of Jesus

Any demonic incisions loose your hold over my life and be purged out of my foundation.

Any life that has been allowed to die through rituals against me arise and strangulate your killers in Jesus Name.

Any power given the mandate to curse and hinder y progress, summersault and die, in the name of Jesus.

Any shrine malpractice to stop my future, backfire in Jesus Name.

Any wrong exposures to sex loose your hold over my life and be purged out of my foundation.

Arrow of unconscious curses die in the name of Jesus.

Arrows of evil limitation operating in my life, come out with all your root and die, in the name of Jesus.

Bless and thank God for His mercy and grace upon you.

blessed with love, joy and peace throughout our lives and that Jesus will be the King of our lives.

Blood of Jesus separate me and my household from every evil dedication.

Blood sucking power or Vampire power, I am not your candidate, die in Jesus Name.

Break and loose yourself from every inherited course in Jesus name.

By the blood of Jesus Christ, I bind the activity of any evil spirits in Jesus' name. We claim the full armour of God (Ephesians 6:10-18).

By the blood of Jesus Christ, I bind the activity of any evil spirits in Jesus' name. We claim the full armour of God (Ephesians 6:10-18).

curses against my life, in the mighty name of Jesus.

Curses by day and by night shall not stand in my life in Jesus name.

Curses of darkness tying down my progress, break and burn to ashes, in the name of Jesus.

Curses of wickedness of my mother's house, break by fire.

Declare your decision to remain faithful to Jesus all the days of your life.

Every ancestral embargo, be lifted; and let good things begin to break forth in my life and in my family, in the name of Jesus.

Every ancestral evil altar prospering against me, be dashed against the Rock of Ages, in Jesus name.

Every arrow of rising and falling jump out and backfire, in the name of Jesus..

Every arrow of sickness that can lead to death fired into my life, come out and go back to the sender.

Every Balaam hired to curse me, die after the order of Balaam.

Every blood powered on the ground shall not eat me up in Jesus Name.

Every curse controlling my life, break and die, in the name of Jesus.

Every curse keeping stagnancy in place in my life, break by fire.

Every curse militating against my prosperity and fulfillment of my goals, Be destroyed in the name of Jesus.

Every curse militating against my prosperity, and the fulfillment of my goals, BE DESTROYED! In the name of Jesus.

Every curse of "Thou shall not excel," break and release me.

Every curse of moving from battle to battle, die in Jesus Name.

Every curse of rising and falling operating in my life, break and die.

Every curse of sickness and infirmity, break by the blood of Jesus.

Every curse of tragedy, break and die.

Every curse of untimely death over my life and family, break and die.

Every curse of vagabond, break and release me, in the name of Jesus.

Every curse pronounced inwardly against my destiny, break in the name of Jesus.

Every curse that I have brought into my life through disobedience and ignorance, break by fire in the name of Jesus Christ.

Every curse that I have brought into my life through ignorance and disobedience, break by fire in the name of Jesus.

Every curse, evil covenant and all inherited problems passed down to the
children sho uld be cancelled, in the name of Jesus.

Every darkness planted in my foundation, scatter, in the name of Jesus.

Every decision, vow or promise made by my forefathers contrary to my divine destiny, loose your hold by fire, in the name of Jesus.

Every destructive power that has entered into my reproductive organs be removed by fire.

Every evil ancestral habit and weakness of moral failures manifesting in my life, loose your grip and release me now, in Jesus' name.

Every evil ancestral river flowing down to my generation, I cut you off, in the name of Jesus.

Every evil animal representing me and being used to afflict my life, I separate myself from you and I set you on fire, in the name of Jesus.

Every evil animal representing me and being used to afflict my life, I separate myself from you and I set you on fire, in the name of Jesus.

Every evil influence and activity of strange women on my children should
be nullified, in the name of Jesus.

Every evil label causing problems for me in life, catch fire, roast.

Every evil personality following me around die, and release me.

Every evil soul tie covenant between me and ……… (Put the full name) break and release me.

Every foundation of family strongmen rooted in my dreams, visions and destiny, be uprooted in the name of Jesus.

Every foundational arrester, be arrested, in the name of Jesus.

Every foundational confusion, die, in the name of Jesus.

Every foundational familiar spirit, I bind you and cast you out, in the name of Jesus.

Every foundational marine power, bow, in the name of Jesus.

Every generational curse of God resulting from the sin of idolatry on my forefathers, loose your hold, in the name of Jesus.

Every generational curse working against my life, break and die.

Every generational curse working against my life, break and die.

Every grip of the evil consequences of the ancestral worship of my forefathers' god over my life and ministry, break by fire, in the name of Jesus.

Every gun of witchcraft shooting at me, backfire in Jesus Name.

Every hold of any sacrifice ever offered in my family or on my behalf, I break your power in my life, in the name of Jesus.

Every legal ground of devil is null against our lives terminate now

Every legal ground that ancestral/guardian spirits have in my life, be destroyed by the blood of Jesus.

Every mountain on my way to success and victory, be removed in Jesus' name!

Every Occult power harassing my life with evil curses, die with your curses, in the name of Jesus.

Every power assigned to turn my life upside down, release me and die.

Every power binding me and my destiny, release me and let me go.

Every power magnetizing physical and spiritual curses to me, I raise the blood of Jesus against you and I challenge you by fire in the name of Jesus.

Every power supervising curses in my life, fall down and die.

Every power that has established evil authority in my family, die in Jesus Name.

Every problem attached to my family name, be neutralized, in the name of Jesus.

Every rage and rampage of ancestral and family spirits resulting from my being born again, be quenched by the liquid fire of God, in the name of Jesus.

Every sacrifice that has prevailed against me die.

Every satanic agenda of the wicked for my life, scatter by fire, in the name of Jesus.

Every Satanic power monitoring my destiny, be paralyzed b y fire, in the name of Jesus.

Every scorpion in my foundation, die, in the name of Jesus.

Every seed of witchcraft in my foundation, die, in the name of Jesus.

Every serpent in my foundation, die, in the name of Jesus.

Every star hijacker from my place of birth, receive divine madness, in the name of Jesus.

Every strange judgments that is flying over my life council in Jesus name

Every strange kingdom ruling my life and destiny scatter by fire

Every stronghold of family strongman upon my spirit, soul and body, be shattered to pieces in the name of Jesus.

Every stubborn curse controlling my life break and die, in the name of Jesus.

Every stubborn curse controlling my life break and die, in the name of Jesus.

Every unconscious evil soul-tie and covenant with the spirits of my dead grandfather, grandmother, occult uncles, aunties, custodian of family gods/oracles/shrines, be broken by the blood of Jesus.

Every ungodly convention holding for my sake scatter to desolation, in the name of Jesus.

Every unspoken curse against my life, break, in the name of Jesus.

Every unspoken curse against my life, family and business, break in the name of Jesus Christ.

Every voice from any evil dedication speaking against my life, be terminated by fire.

Every weapon of the wicked assigned against my life, backfire in the name of Jesus.

Evil covenants keeping evil dedication in place in my life, break by the blood of Jesus.

Evil dedication speaking against my life and destiny, break and die by the power in the blood of Jesus.

Family idols, receive the consuming fire of God, in the name of Jesus.

Father God, turn every curse I brought upon myself to blessings in Jesus' name.

Father Lord restore back to me everything that I have lost as a result of evil dedication.

Father Lord, let the blood of Jesus wash me all of evil mark and make me clean in
Christ name.

Father Lord, turn all my self-imposed curses to blessings in Jesus' name

Father to son curses, mother to daughter curses in my life, die in Jesus Name.

Father, destroy anything in my children preventing them from doing Your
will, in the name of Jesus.

Father, disconnect me from the frequency of my father or my parents.

Father, let the fire of the Holy Ghost enter into my blood stream and cleanse my system, in Jesus name.

Father, Lord, turn all my self-imposed curses to blessings, in Jesus name

Generational liability in my family line, break in Jesus Name.

God arise and change the rules for my sake, in the name of Jesus.

God arise and turn every challenge assigned to make me weep to joy, in Jesus name.

I arrest the spiritual soldiers of any family strongmen watching over the affairs of my life in the name of Jesus.

I ask You to forgive me or my ancestors for any sin that has exposed me to a curse (name any specific sin that you are aware of.) I receive Your forgiveness and I choose to forgive those who've sinned against me (name these people).

I bind every spirit blinding their minds from receiving the glorious light of
the Gospel our Lord Jesus Christ, in the name of Jesus.

I bind every spirit contrary to the spirit of God preventing me from enjoying
my children, in the name of Jesus.

I break all curses or vows that have ever been spoken over me from my mother and father and from all generational curses that have been spoken over anyone in my ancestry all the way back to Adam and Eve.

I break all generational curses of pride, lust, perversion, rebellion, witchcraft, idolatry, poverty, sickness, infirmity, disease, rejection, fear, confusion, addiction, death, and destruction in the name of Jesus.

I break all the curses of deformity, infirmity and sickness in my family back to ten generations on both sides of my family in the name of Jesus.

I break and cancel every curse placed upon me by my parents, in the name of Jesus.

I break and cancel every curse, spell, hex, enchantment, bewitchment, incantation placed upon me by my involvement with evil association, in the name of Jesus.

I break and cancel every inherited curse and every curse placed upon me by my
parents, in the name of Jesus.

I break and cancel every inherited curse, in the name of Jesus.

I break and loose myself from every from of demonic bewitchment in the name of Jesus.

I break and loose myself from every inherited evil curse in Jesus name.

I break and loosen myself from every inherited evil curse in Jesus' name.

I break and renounce every conscious and unconscious association with close evil
friends, lodge, idols and familiar spirits, in the name of Jesus.

I break and revoke every blood and soul-tie covenant and the yokes attached to
them, in the name of Jesus.

I break and revoke every blood and soul-tie covenant and yokes attached to them, in the name of Jesus.

I break any curse contrary to child bearing transferred to me by any boyfriend/girlfriend in Jesus' name.

I break any curse of rejection from the womb or illegitimacy that may be in my family back to ten generations on both sides of the family in the name of Jesus..

I break any ungodly ties that still bind me to anyone in my life who's ever hurt or disappointed me or to whom I have related in an ungodly way. (Name these people as you break the unhealthy bonding and 'soul ties'.)

I break every covenant entered into with the spirit husband or wife and kill all the
children between us, in the name of Jesus.

I break every covenants and oaths, made consciously or unconsciously, and
binding me with any association, in the name of Jesus.

I break every covenants entered into with Jezebel spirits, water spirits and Queen of
the coast spirits, in the name of Jesus.

I break every curse associated with every evil dedication operating in my life, by the power in the blood of Jesus.

I break every curse of automatic failure mechanism working in the name of Jesus.

I break every demonic circle in my life, in the name of Jesus.

I break every evil covenant and initiation and command their ungodly powers to
release me, in the name of Jesus.

I break myself loose from every evil curses and covenants, in the name of Jesus.

I break self-imposed stagnancy and limitations in the name of Jesus Christ.

I break the yoke of any family strongman upon my life in the name of Jesus.

I bring the Blood of Jesus over every evil claim from the family strongman over my life in the name of Jesus.

I cancel every curse of untimely death sent against me in the name of Jesus.

I cancel every curse of untimely death sent against me, in the name of Jesus.

I cancel the consequence of every evil name attached to my life.

I cancel the effect of all former satanic benefits upon my life, in the name of Jesus.

I cancel the evil dedication of my name to any evil family strongman in the name of Jesus.

I challenge my body, soul and spirit with the fire of God, in the name of Jesus.

I claim back any territory of my life handed over to Satan, in the name of Jesus.

I come against Jezebel spirit, water spirit and Queen of the coast in the name of
Jesus.

I come out from every divination, enchantment, evil altar and imagination of the mighty, in the name of Jesus.

I command all foundational strongman attached to my life to be paralysed in the name of Jesus.

I command all foundational strongmen attached to my life to be paralyzed in the name of Jesus.

I command all the enemy of God in my life, husband/wife, family to carry their entire problems today, in Jesus name

I command all ungodly powers to release me, in the name of Jesus.

I command every door open to satanic invasion in my life to be shut now, in the
name of Heus

I command every satanic embargo placed upon my life to catch fire and burn to ashes NOW in the name of Jesus Christ,

I command in Jesus' name, with the heavenly authority that every curse pronounced over the life of 'X' (your full name) is cancelled.

I command the fire of god to roast and burn to ashes every evil bird, snake or any
other animal attached to my life by evil association, in the name of Jesus.

I command the fire of God to roast the forces of infirmity, sickness, hindrance and
failure in my life, in the name of Jesus.

I command the hunter of fire of god to burn to ashes the marriage certificate,
wedding gown, ring and all other materials used for the marriage.

I declare and decree that there shall be no reinforcement, regrouping and counterattack of curses against my life, in the mighty name of Jesus.

I declare my body, soul and spirit a-no-go-area for all evil spirits, in the name of Jesus

I declare that my descendants will receive blessing and favor from this day forward. That we will be blessed with love, joy and peace throughout our lives and that Jesus will be the King of our lives. Amen.

I declare that my descendants will receive blessings and favor from this day forward. That we will be

I declare that there shall be no barrenness in my life.

I destroy by fire, every boundary the enemy has marked down for me in Jesus' name.

I destroy from my life, every cycle of failure, disappointments, sickness, and frustration in Jesus' name.

I destroy from my life, every cycle of failure, disappointments, sickness and frustration in Jesus' name.

I destroy from my life, every cycle of failure, disappointments, sickness, and frustration in Jesus' name.

I do once and for all release myself from the power and authorities of any curse.

I especially pray for the blessings given unto all humans at creation - that of fruitfulness, multiplication, and dominion.

I especially pray for the blessings given unto all humans at creation - that of fruitfulness, multiplication and dominion.

I loose myself from curses, spells, bewitchment and evil domination- of evil
societies, in the name of Jesus.

I loose myself from every other spirits which is not the spirit of Christ in the name
of Jesus.

I out bless all the effects of the curse and by the power of God, we turn the curse into a blessing.

I pray all these things in the authority of the name of Jesus and give You thanks and praise, Lord, that all these things are done.

I pray for the blessings of Abraham that are ours in Christ (Galatians 3:8-29) to be appropriated by X and given to him/her in abundance.

I pray today, the entire evil standard laid down by your parents will not be your portion in Jesus' name.

I pronounce blessings over my life to replace the curses that have been broken.

I pull down our any organ from my body stored in satanic banks, in Jesus name.

I purge myself of all evil food I had eaten in any of the evil association with the
blood of Jesus.

I purge myself of all the evil covenants and curses, in the name of Jesus.

I purge myself of all the evil foods I have eaten in the evil world with the blood of Jesus and purify myself with the fire of the Holy Ghost, in the name of Jesus.

I purge out with the blood of Jesus every evil material and break the head of snake
deposed in my body by the spirit husband and wife, in the name of Jesus.

I receive the mandate to release my children from the prison of any
strongman, in the name of Jesus.

I recover every good thing stolen by ancestral evil spirits from my forefathers, my immediate family and myself, in Jesus' name.

I refuse to die the death of an unbeliever, in the name of Jesus.

I reject every curse of miscarriage and premature birth in my family.

I reject the calendar of death prepared for my divine potentials, in the name of Jesus.

I release my children from the bondage of any evil domination, in the
name of Jesus.

I release my life from every evil dedication by the power in the blood of Jesus.

I release myself from any inherited bondage and limitations in the name of Jesus.

I release myself from any inherited bondage in the name of Jesus.

I release myself from demonic pollution emanating from my past involvement in any demonic religion in the name of Jesus.

I release myself from every ancestral demonic pollution in the name of Jesus.

I release myself from every demonic pollution emanating from my parents' religion in the name of Jesus.

I release myself from every inherited disease in the name of Jesus.

I release myself from the grip of any problem transferred into my life from the womb in Jesus name.

I release myself from the grip of any problem transferred into my life from the womb in the name of Jesus.

I release myself from the grip of every ancestral spirits in the name of Jesus.

I remove my life from the agenda of my household witchcraft, in the name of Jesus.

I remove my name from the roaster of dark agents in my family, in the name of Jesus.

I renounce all attitudes of reliance upon man and the flesh. I resolve to put my trust solely in the Lord, my God.

I renounce and divorce my marriage with the spirit husband/wife, in the name of
Jesus.

I renounce any and all contact with the occult and promise to destroy and occult objects that I may possess. (Name the specific occult involvement.)

I renounce any and all curses that I've spoken against others, whether knowingly or unknowingly: gossip, bitter words, anger, and judgment. I break the authority of any such occult power in my life.

I renounce any and all patterns of stinginess with finances that I or my ancestors have engaged. I resolve to be obedient to the Lord in the area of tithes and offerings.

I renounce any and all self-inflicted curses that I've pronounced on myself, and I break those patterns from my heart and tongue.

I renounce any and all sexual sins, and I break the power of pornography that may have a hold of me.

I renounce any and all unholy covenants in which I or my ancestors have been involved (name them).

I renounce any ungodly beliefs, traditions, rituals, or customs that my people may have followed or acted upon.

I renounce my association with all evil association and pull myself out of them, in
the name of Jesus.

I renounce the behavior of any relative in our family background who has lived more for the world, than for God.

I renounce the behavior of any relative in our family background who has lived more for the world, than for God. I renounce any ungodly beliefs, traditions, rituals, or customs that my people may have followed or acted upon. I repent of those family members who sought to fulfill the selfishness of their desires, and those who have perverted God's righteousness for I myself choose to serve God and live by His ways.

I renounce the curse and all its effects. I break the curse and all its power in the name of Jesus Christ of Nazareth.

I repent for every relative connected to my family ancestry who has deliberately, or without spiritual wisdom sinned against my Lord, or His people.

I repent for every relative connected to my family's ancestry who has deliberately, or without spiritual wisdom sinned against my Lord, or His people.

I repent on behalf of those family members who sought to fulfill the selfishness of their desires, and those who have perverted God's righteousness for I myself choose to serve God and live by His ways.

I resign my position in any of these evil associations and withdraw my services and responsibilities, in the name of Jesus.

I vomit every evil consumption that I have been fed with as a child in the name of Jesus

I withdraw any mandate given to any power to curse me by the power in the blood of Jesus.

I withdraw any part of my body and blood deposited on evil alters and satanic banks, in the name of Jesus.

I withdraw my pictures, image and inner- man from the alters and control of evil
associations, in the name of Jesus.

I withdrawn and cancel my name from the registers of these evil associations with
the blood of Jesus.

Let all evil influences by demonic friends by demonic friends clear away, in
the name of Jesus.

Let all good things burned alive come forth now, in the name of Jesus.

Let all spirit of stubbornness, pride and disrespect for parents flee from
their lives, in the name of Jesus.

Let any rod of the wicked rising up against my family line be rendered impotent for my sake in the name of Jesus.

Let every association and agreement between my children and my
enemies be scattered, in the name of Jesus.

Let every property of Jezebel spirit, water spirits and Queen of the coast in my
possession, receive the fire of God and burn to ashes, in the name of Jesus.

Let every spirit of Balaam hired to curse my progress fall down and die in the name of Jesus.

Let every witchcraft curse go back to the sender sevenfold in the name of Jesus.

Let God arise and all the enemies of my home be scattered.

Let God arise and let all foundational witchcraft scatter, in the, name of Jesus.

Let the angels of God arrest every negative words spoken against my destiny, in the name of Jesus.

Let the blood of Jesus correct any inherited defect in my body in the name of Jesus.

Let the blood of Jesus flush out from my system every inherited satanic deposit in the name of Jesus.

Let the blood of Jesus wash my name away from the notebook of dark powers, in
the name of Jesus.

Let the fire of God descend on satanic coven and burn to ashes the spirit
husband/wife operating in my life, in the name of Jesus.

Let the fire of the Holy Ghost fall on me and begin to burn every deposit and mark
of the enemy, in the name of Jesus.

Let the habitation of the strongmen behind my problem receive total destruction, in the mighty name of Jesus.

Let the name of Jesus terrifies all evil association.

Let the Pharaoh in my place of birth fall down and die, in the name of Jesus.

Let the power of the Holy Ghost plant my feet in Christ Jesus, in the name of Jesus.

Let the precious blood of Jesus cleanse my body, soul and spirit from evil marks,
in the name of Jesus.

Let the sword of fire begin to cut off every evil parental attachment in the mighty name of Jesus.

Let the thunder of God strike the altar of family strongmen in the name of Jesus.

Let the water of life flush out every unwanted stranger in my life in Jesus name

Let the whirlwind scatter every vessel of infirmity in the name of Jesus.

Let the wickedness of the family strongman be overturned in the mighty name of Jesus.

Let your deliverance hand be stretched out upon my life now in Jesus' name; and let your healing hand be stretched out upon my life now in the name of Jesus.

Let your miracle hand be stretched out upon my life now in the name of Jesus.

Lord Jesus, hold me tight and effect immediately break-through in every area of
my life, in the name of Jesus.

Lord Jesus, walk back into every second of my life and deliver me where I need deliverance heal me where I need healing, transforms me where I need transformation.

Lord my father, lift up my head this year in the name of Jesus.

Lord my Father; take over my battles in the name of Jesus.

Lord my God, direct my path this year in the name of Jesus.

Lord, accelerate my divine honor by fire, in the name of Jesus.

Lord, anoint me to pray without ceasing.

Lord, anoint my eyes and my ears that they may see and hear wondrous things from heaven.

Lord, arise and promote me by fire, in the name of Jesus.

Lord, arise and swallow every rage of poverty designed for me in your power, in the name of Jesus.

Lord, arise with your mighty and make a way for me where there is no way.

Lord, arise with your mighty and outstretched and make a way for me where there is no way.

Lord, begin to clean away from my life all that does not reflect you.

Lord, break down every evil foundation of my life, and rebuild a now one or Christ
the Rock, in the name of Jesus.

Lord, bring light into all the dark rooms in my soul.

Lord, bring light into the shadows of my life.

Lord, by the blood of Jesus, uproot every seed of limitation in my life in Jesus' name.

Lord, convert my disgrace to grace in the name of Jesus.

Lord, deliver me from the lies I tell myself.

Lord, empower me to resist satan that he would flee.

Lord, forgive me all my ancestral sexual sins in the name of Jesus.

Lord, forgive me for all my ancestral sexual sins in the name of Jesus.

Lord, I thank you for the victory that You have won for me today.

Lord, let Your electric love flow into my life.

Lord, let Your purpose for my life be fulfilled.

Lord, liberate my spirit to follow the leading of the Holy Spirit.

Lord, make me attractive to prosperity.

Lord, make my mouth bigger than enemies', in the name of Jesus.

Lord, make my mouth bigger than my enemies', in the name of Jesus.

Lord, move my life forward by fire in the name of Jesus.

Lord, nullify the evil influence of family strongman upon my life in the name of Jesus.

Lord, re-arrange my situation to defeat and disgrace my enemies.

Lord, rearrange my situation to glorify Your name.

Lord, remove from me all the curses placed upon my ancestral families as a result of their evil associations, involvement, etc, in the name of Jesus.

Lord, restore me to your original destiny for my life.

Lord, send your axe of fire to the foundation of my life and destroy every evil plantation.

Lord, speak deliverance to any bondage situation in my life.

Lord, terminate the life of all sicknesses in my life in the name of Jesus.

Lord, uproot the root cause of any chronic failures.

Lord, wash and cleanse me from past wounds and scars.

Mention their names one by one and tell the Lord, what you want them to
become.

My children will not become mis-directed arrows, in the name of Jesus.

My destiny, rise up from every valley of limitation today and begin to move forward in Jesus' name.

My father, divinely separate me from every friendly and unfriendly friend serving as a channel of limitation for my life in Jesus' name.

My good and my destiny that was locked away from my life, I unlock you with the key of David in the hands of Jesus Christ and command you, come forth and locate me NOW!!! in the name of Jesus Christ.

My kingship garments taking by my enemies return them to today and die

My life, home and destiny is not for sale in the name of Jesus, in the name of Jesus.

My trouble, you are in trouble by fire in the name of Jesus.

Negative dreams shall not come to pass in my life in the name of Jesus.

Negative power from my foundation assigned to kill my destiny, die in Jesus' name

No reinforcement, and no regrouping for all the problems that have gone in Jesus' name

Oh Lord, let the anointing of the Holy Spirit break every yoke of backwardness in my life.

Oil of favour, baptize my life in the name of Jesus.

Owners of evil load, hear the word of the lord: carry your load in my life in the name of Jesus.

Parental curses placed upon my life, break and release me now.

Power of darkness holding my glory, release me in the name of Jesus Christ.

Powers assigned to kill me before my glory manifest die in Jesus Name.

Powers that want me to die the death of another person, die in Jesus Name.

Pronounce blessings over your life to replace the curses that you have just broken.

Quencher of deliverance, die in the name of Jesus.

Renounce and break every inherited evil covenant, in Jesus name.

Round the circles covenant, break in the name of Jesus.

Satanic problems anchor, be roasted in the name of Jesus.

Sickness, pain and weakness, get out of my system in the name of Jesus.

Spirit of the living God, quicken the whole of my being in the name of Jesus.

spirits, i. inherited spirit husbands/wives, j. spirits inside /under sacred rocks / hills,

Territorial powers of this city shall not break my neck in Jesus Name.

Thank God for making provision for deliverance from any form of bondage

Thank you, Lord for breaking every curse operating in my life.

The gates of the ancestral demon working against my divine goal in life is broken by the power of Jesus in the name of Jesus.

The legal ground of the enemy positioning me for attacks, die in Jesus' name

The power manipulating and blocking my progress, receive the judgment of God now in Jesus' name

The tree of family strongmen in my life, be cut down in the name of Jesus.

Thou evil powers of the night, be humbled and disgraced in Jesus' name

Unbroken curses troubling my star, break in the name of Jesus.

Voices of strangers, assigned to destroy my destiny die in the name of Jesus.

Where is the Lord God of Elijah? Arise and make me a mysterious wonder in Jesus' name

Where no member of family has reached, O' Lord, take me there by fire in Jesus' name.

Where others are failing in my family, I shall excel by fire, in the name of Jesus.

Wherever they have risen up against, Oh! God of Elijah rise up against them in Jesus Name.

Wicked broadcasters of my divine goodness fall down and die, in the name of Jesus.

Wicked curses of my father's house, break and release me now.

Witchcraft agents raining incantations on me, carry your load and die.

Witchcraft curses harassing my life and destiny, break.

Yokes that do not want me to lift my head, break in the name of Jesus.

You (mention the name of the child), I dissociate you from any conscious or unconscious demonic groupings or involvement in the name of Jesus.

You evil night workers, I crush your powers in the name of Jesus.

You human powers behind my problems, be removed from the face of the earth now in Jesus' name.

You inward curses, militating against my virtues, break, in the name of Jesus.

You my legs, receive fire and move me to my place of breakthrough in Jesus' name.

You powers of the night, I command the power of God to pursue you in the name of Jesus.

You powers of the night, I command the sword of the Lord to slay you in the name of Jesus.

You problem propagators and problem prolongers, be paralyzed in the name of Jesus.

You progress diverters from my past, I damage your weapon of divination by fire, in the name of Jesus.

You Queen of coast, let your water cry dry up, in the name of Jesus.

You spirit of confusion, loose your hold over my life in the name of Jesus.

You spirit of confusion, lose your hold over my life in the name of Jesus.

You spirit of infirmities, sickness and failure, release me, in the name of Jesus.

You spiritual cannibals, vomit my blood and flesh now in the name of Jesus.

You stubborn pursuer, I command your ways to be slippery and I ask the angels of God to pursue you in Jesus' name.

You the enemies of my career, be paralyzed in the name of Jesus.

You the spirit of grave and death, be scattered in the name of Jesus.

You water spirit, I command your water to be polluted with the acid of God, in the
name of Jesus.

You, my legs, receive fire and move me to my place of a breakthrough in Jesus' name.

You, spiritual cannibals, vomit my blood and flesh now in the name of Jesus.

I declare and decree that there shall be no reinforcement, regrouping and counterattack of curses against my life, in the mighty name of Jesus.

Thank you Lord for breaking every curse operating in my life.

Pronounce blessings over your life to replace the curses that you have just broken.

As you mention each of the items listed below repeat three times "Break, break, break, and release me, in the name of Jesus."

a.   Evil manipulation of the placenta

b.   Evil pots stealing from me

c.   Book of generational failure.

d.   Yoke of forest spirits

e.   Yoke of familiar spirits

f.   Mantle of witchcraft spirit

g.   Curse of rejection

i.   Curse of hatred

j.   Curse of untimely death

k.   Curse of loneliness

l.   Curse of isolation

m.   Curse of declination

n.   Curse of sickness and infirmity

o.   Curse of "It shall not be well with you"

p.   Curse of barrenness

q.   Curse of non-achievement

As you mention each of the items listed below, repeat seven times

"I reject you, in the name of Jesus."

a.   Tears and sorrow

b.   ancestral loneliness

c.   shame

d.   reproach

e.   disappointment

f.   disgrace

g.   poverty

h.   rejection

i.   untimely death

j.   sickness

k.   stagnancy

l.   Affliction

ABOUT THE AUTHOR

Joel Odunayo Daramola whom God raised from grass to grace, has pioneered many parishes in The Redeemed Christian Church of God.

Currently: As Assistance Provincial Pastor Admin in Lagos province 37.

A graduate of The Redeemed Christian Bible College (RCBC), School of Disciple (SOD) and Institute of Leadership.

He holds a B.A. (Ed) in Guidance and Counseling from the prestigious University of Lagos (UNILAG).

He is a teacher who is registered with the teacher's registration council of Nigeria (TRCN)

A trained R & A Engineer (thermodynamics) with over 30 years' experience.

He is the CEO, Ayo-Technical Services (ATS). & Vision Link For You and I.

He is the host of Power Service (a weekly breakthrough and deliverance service) for over two decades.

A prolific writer, author of many books; a respected Evangelist, a gifted prophet with vast insight into the word of God.

Publisher of the Monthly Journal: "VISION LINK" for more than 20 years.

He has the vision to challenge young people to actualize their potentials in life.

His mandate is to spread the word of God, raise disciples, and build them to maturity for the perfection of saints through God's empowerment.

A prolific speaker, dexterous writer and a leading voice in Ministry and Leadership circles,

He is sought as a Conference speaker across the globe. His ministry is in high demand by both denominational and non-denominational ministries alike as his ability to engage people with God's word and effective prayer

He is passionate about raising people who are thoroughly steeped in Kingdom values and very relevant in the Secular world.

He believes that Christians should be able to influence society with kingdom principles.

His fine blend of excellence and spirituality has made him stand out from the pack.

He believes God has a plan for everybody and that God can take the most unlikely and use him powerfully.

A Youth leader, an administrator, entrepreneur and motivational speaker with a global vision.

A motivational speaker for over two decades. He has organized seminars and conferences to inspire the Youths in schools and Church for

Nation building, Vision discovery and career advancement. His fine blend of excellence and spirituality has made him stand out from the pack, he believes that God has a plan for everybody and that God can make use of anyone powerfully.

He has published many books; Sounds of the abundance of rain; At the darkest hour; Are you passing through? Destined for greatness but tied down among others.

He is happily married to Pastor (Mrs.) C.O. Daramola and their union is blessed with four Children: Power, Queen, Excellence and Great.

Emails: pastordara@yahoo.com & visionlinkdara1@gmail.com

Phone & WhatsApp +2348033275896.

Facebook: Joel Odunayo Daramola

Websites: www.visionlink4u.com